Claire,

I wish   in
your lif
family a   osper
and flourish forever.

Shouting from the Summits

Best Wishes,

Kala Ramachandran

29/05/2017

Clink
Street

London | New York

Published by Clink Street Publishing 2016

Copyright © 2016

First edition.

ISBN: 978-1-911110-55-2
eBook ISBN: 978-1-911110-56-9

ACKNOWLEDGEMENTS

Shouting from the Summits is a result of my personal life journey - from dealing with a stammer at a young age to preparing to conquer Everest. I have had to be bold and courageous, whether that's preparing for the climb of a lifetime or gaining the confidence to overcome the fear of speaking.

My life has been an adventure of finding my voice through my many climbing expeditions. I have made many special friends along the way; they are now a big part of my life. They cried when I failed and cheered when I picked myself up - for this I thank them.

My special thanks to my family; especially my late Dad, Ramachandran Gopal; my Mum Leela Raghupathi; my sister Alli and brothers Saravanan and Elanggoh.

Thank you to my childhood friend, Malathy, with whom I shared so many early adventures before I moved to London. To my two great friends - Sugerla and Kumari - who encouraged and listened passionately to all climbing stories each time I returned from expeditions. To my fellow climbers Mr Chong, Uncle Chong, Uncle Yap, Groover and Bala, all of whom had faith in me. To my late Auntie Laxmi, my Auntie Gomez; my Uncle Raju and his wife; and my Uncle Sundram.

My utmost thanks to Leys Geddes who has been the greatest supporter ever since I openly talked about stammering. Without his support this book would not have been possible.

My further thanks to Warren McDonald, who never failed to reply to my messages, even though I have never met him.

I would like to extend my thanks to Neena A Patel, Lisa, Anu, Caroline Davies, Janet Baidoo, Gwen Shonubi, Besty and my colleagues for their unwavering support.

To Aleida and Andrea McAuley for looking after my boys whilst I was busy training and climbing.

To my publishers Gareth and Hayley, and my editor Lucy - who have been very patient in working on my story.

With further thanks to Khoo Swee Chiow who introduced me to world class mountaineers such as Jason Black and Jing Luo, with whom I have stayed in touch since my return from Mt Aconcagua. And to my fellow climbers who were part of my many expeditions.

To my two sons, Reganathan and Kevinathan for giving their mummy the time at home to finish this story with the little time she had. You two have pushed mummy further, to continue to aspire for an ever-greater life for us all.

Finally, to everyone else - you know who you are.

MY BACKGROUND

My Family

My paternal grandfather, Gopal, was brought from India to Malaya by the British as a 'Mandor': he supervised rubber tappers. My grandmother also was from India and was a very kind lady.

My father, Ramachandran, was born in 1940 in Rengomalay, Kluang, Johore. He was disabled. His right leg was shorter and thinner than the other leg. As a result he limped.

Dad went to school at a late age. On his first day, returning from school, he was walking along when suddenly he heard the loud noise of a car just behind him and he fell to the ground. His writing board and chalks were broken. He could not stand up and was crying on the side of the road. The car driver was English and the chief of the village. He got down from his car and picked my dad up and comforted him not to cry, and then he drove away. My dad went home and told his mum about the incident and she hugged him to comfort him too. The next day he went to school with no writing board and chalks. His teacher noticed this and, unexpectedly, the English chief visited his classroom to hand a new writing board and chalks to Dad. He was very delighted and that unexpected memorable incident stayed in his memories for the rest of his life.

He was placed in Year 2 in English school but he could not read or write English. His teacher made him stand on his chair and his classmates laughed and bullied him. His teacher took him to see the school's head teacher. The head teacher asked why he did not want to read. He answered, "I don't know how to read A, B, C, and how can I study at Year 2?" The next day he was placed in Year 1, where his younger brother was studying. His family moved from their village to another village after his dad lost his 'Mandor' job and this disrupted his studies. His mum and dad had a dairy farm and vegetable patches. They sold cows' milk and vegetables to raise their family. He lost his father on 22.10.1956 and he then went to work during the daytime to support his family.

Nevertheless, he never stopped studying. He was very ambitious and to study further he cycled to town to attend night classes. He became a temporary teacher from 1961 to 1963; he became a qualified teacher in 1966 and commenced his teaching career in 1967 in Carmen estate in Pahang. However, with a lot of family burden on his shoulders, he was very depressed. He was refused by his uncle to marry his sweetheart. As a result he could not sleep for two consecutive weeks and became mentally ill: schizophrenia. However, he always took medication and I have never seen him having any psychotic episodes or mental breakdown. He was a self-motivator. The only problem was that he was such a hot tempered man if he did not have enough sleep or if he did not take a nap during the afternoon. He had diabetes at a young age too. Also he was a role model for many families in Malaysia, even after his death and up until today. My dad spoke highly about his mother to us.

My mother, Leela, who comes from a large family, has very little formal education. Her father, Raghupathi, was born in 1917 in Velur, India. My grandfather and his friends were brought to the Kelan estate, Malaya by the British. He was a 'Toddy Drawer'. He climbed very tall coconut trees to cut the flowers of the tree and fasten an earthenware pot to the flower stump to collect sap. The sap is white liquid which is known as 'toddy drink'. My grand-father supported his family by collecting and selling toddy. My maternal grandmother was a keen reader. They had five children and my mother was the third in her family.

One day in 1954, the knife Raghupathi used fell off and ripped the rope that harnessed him. He fell to the ground and injured his back. He was hospitalised immediately at Johore Bahru General Hospital and died after eight months of being bedridden in the hospital. My mother's family suffered financially and therefore she had to stop her formal education at the age of twelve, and worked as a rubber tapper to support her family income.

Mum and Dad married in 1969. My elder brother, Saravanan, is the first in the family, my sister, Alli, is the second, I am the third and brother Elanggoh is the last child.

Mother was a housewife for few years of her married life. She dedicated her entire life to making sure dad had enough sleep and that his schizophrenia did not affect his daily life.

Childhood

My childhood memories go back to when I was four years plus, when we were living at Taman Pandan just seven miles from Johore Bahru town, which is the capital of Johore. At that time, we lived in our own big house with a large front garden. I remember my mother's tummy was bulging when she was heavily pregnant with my younger brother. I remember the day one of my distant neigh-bours told us my mother had given birth to a boy. I was delighted. I remember carrying him and putting him to sleep next to me when he was a little baby.

When we were growing up, we used to play together with other kids.

One particular event has disturbed my mind throughout my

My first photo, aged 4

My parents' wedding

A group photo from a school trip with Mt Austin Primary School students, I am at the second row, 5th from the right, behind me was my Teacher Mr. Stephen

1991, the Kuala Tembeling jetty with my camping team mates, waiting for the boat to head to Kuala Tahan jetty

1997, on Low's Peak, Mount Kinabalu (4101 m) with Datuk Magendran, the first Malaysian Everest summiteer

life. There was this old Chinese man who worked in a timber company just further down behind our house. Four of us used to play there with other kids and I had seen him taking my younger brother with him and he would pull down my brother's underpants. My younger brother used to cry at that age. I did not know how to tell my mother and father about that. I simply hated that man and tried to avoid playing at the timber company. No one else said anything of that to my parents either. Now, being a parent myself, I feel a child should have freedom to express their joy, frustration and imagination.

School

My dad sent me to city kindergarten when I was six. But I vomited throughout the journey during my first week and the van driver refused to take me any more. So I did not have the choice of attending a kindergarten and had to accept being at home a year before going to primary school at the age of seven. All my siblings had kindergarten education.

My dad asked me one day which school I wanted to attend. All my siblings went to National School, which is Malay medium school. I chose to go to Mount Austin Tamil School, where he was a teacher. I admired my dad for giving me the freedom to choose the school I wanted to go. So, he would drive me and another two kids, who lived near our house, to the primary school. I admired the beauty of rubber trees during our car journey to my village school while dreaming of being a lawyer one day.

Things went wrong when I found out the two kids did not wear underpants when they came to school. I was just over protective towards them, maybe because of what I saw the old Chinese man do to my younger brother. I told the two kids that they would have to pay me ten cents if they came to school without their underpants on. This was a secret side of me which I have never told to anybody until I started to write the story of my life. I feel guilty for doing such bad things as financial punishment for not wearing underpants. The collection of ten cents must have gone on for about three or four weeks and the two kids started to wear their underpants every day after that.

When I was nine years plus, my dad sold our family home in Taman Pandan and bought a new house in Ulu Tiram, where my mum still lives with my older brother and his daughter. Dad bought one bicycle for four of us. I loved cycling until one day I had an accident which caused injuries to my knees and bruises on my arm. Dad somehow did not like me spending time cycling without studying. He complained about me to other schoolteachers. The complaints made me to stop cycling completely.

WHERE IS MY WORD?

My dad had a lot of Tamil story books and we had our own library room at home. He encouraged me to read novels, particularly those written by Dr M Varatharasan. He had a collection of his books. He liked to talk about great world figures like George Bernard Shaw, Winston Churchill, Mahatma Gandhi, Mother Teresa and Abraham Lincoln and spoke highly of Helen Keller. I mainly liked stories like that of Florence Nightingale. I used to think how selfless she was to nurse the wounded soldiers at night time! I read the book so many times during the day. I remember doing school work in the middle of the night under dim light when everyone was sleeping. But I would finish all the school work and was the best in the village school. I read novels under dim light when there was no homework.

One day in 1983, a tall young teacher, Stephen, joined my school. He lived in the same town and Dad gave him a lift in our car. He walked into my classroom and he introduced himself as our new Tamil teacher. He knew I was the brightest child and a teacher's daughter, with some intelligence, so he asked me to stand up and read a passage in Tamil. I stood up proudly. I started to read the passage and all of a sudden a word from the passage would not come out of my mouth. I paused. I perspired. I tried to move my mouth. I said the word. After that it was a fluent reading. I puzzled the whole day thinking, "What has happened to me?!" At that time, I did not even know the words 'stammer' or 'stutter' or 'blocked speech'. We were not encouraged to talk to parents. I thought it might be just a one-off.

The same week, Dad, who was my geography teacher, asked me to read a whole passage from my geography textbook. I stood up and I started to read. Again, a word would not come out. I paused. Then, I read again. Dad raised his voice. I could hear my heart beat so loud in my ears. This time, many words did not come out of my mouth. My heart was racing very fast. He had a cane in his hand. He caned both my arms not just once but for each word that stuck in my mouth. I wept. I trembled. My tears rolled down my cheek. Dad shouted, "Sit down."

I cried throughout the day. I had bruises and red marks on my arms. Mum came back from work but she did not notice any change in me. From that night onwards, I felt in my heart that I belonged somewhere else, a place where people would encourage me to speak about my feelings.

My dad was a very good narrator and storyteller. One day, during geography lesson, Dad mentioned that the first woman to climb Mount Everest, which is the highest mountain in the world (8848 metres), was a Japanese lady – Junko Tabei; and that was what went into my mind. In my mind, I said "I will be the next one." That's where my search for my life purpose began.

STAMMER

I found that words beginning with 'th', 'm', 'n', 'wh', 'v', 'h', 'str', 'r' or 'qu' were very difficult to say. My fear of communication grew day to day. I always could hear my heartbeat louder than my voice. One day, Dad asked me to answer, what was seven times seven? Of course I knew the answer but I could not even say the number forty-nine. He asked me to stand on the chair and asked me again. I still could not move my mouth. He asked me to stretch out my arm and he hit my palm with his wooden ruler. He asked me again and I could not answer. He asked me to stand on the table. The number forty-nine stuck in my mouth. He threw my maths notebook in my face. Again, he punished me in front of my classmates. I was really sad and started to dislike my dad and avoid having conversation with him at home.

As I was bright, Dad entered me into a stage speaking competition. When they called my name, I went onto the stage and faced the crowd. All the judges were sitting in the front row. My dad was one of them. I was about to greet the judges but the word 'judge' stuck in my mouth and it took a minute at least to say the word. After that it was a fluent speech. I won third prize but was pushed back behind in performances every time I spoke on stage.

My school headmaster told me once to make the school proud by becoming one of the top three speakers. In fact, my fear grew intensely every time I stood in front of the school crowd. I did not win any prizes at all. I did not want to see his face when I returned to school. The school board elected me as Head Prefect. I could not lead my school team well, not being be able to express my views because I was frightened my words would stick in my mouth. There was no one to speak to about my stammer. So, I grew up quiet and I was not able to express what I wanted to say simply because of the embarrassment of public caning in front of my classmates. I thought the only way to avoid this embarrassment was via education.

In 1983, Dad gave me a small notebook and asked me to write down one quotation from a world leader each day. The quotations came from a printed Tamil calendar. I must have practised for a few years and used to indulge in those positive thoughts.

I did really well in all school exams, being first from Year 1 to Year 6. What a great achievement in all my written exams!

In 1986 I went to Ulu Tiram Secondary School. In Malaysia, Malay is the national language. As I was from the Tamil stream in primary school, I went to remove class to improve my communication in Malay before going to Form 1 class. My class teacher gave me the Head Class Student role due to my outstanding exam results from my primary school. It meant that I had to stand and greet the teachers when they walked into class and take leading roles too. So many times, I would stand and pause before saying "Good afternoon". My heart would pump fast. My face would feel too hot. I would perspire. Every day was difficult and the whole year was such a difficult one for me. It was very hard to find the motivation and strength to go to school every day.

There was this Indian boy who would try to court me but, unfortunately, as I stammered, I felt too shy even to look into his face. My face always looked to the ground if he passed by me. How was I going to talk to him? So, I stayed put, to focus, to study hard and go to university. I gave up the Head Class Student role when I moved on to a new class in the following year. Again, reading in front of class was the most difficult task for me. I would practise reading textbooks out loud at home before going to school.

The worst thing that happened to me was when I could not say my own name in front of other students when I had to introduce myself to the class. A discipline teacher shouted at me, "Have you got a diamond in your mouth?" I felt really sad and still remember I cried silently in the school toilets. I did not even look at other students' faces. It was such an embarrassing moment simply because everyone would think I had some sort of illness of forgetting my own name. I thought the gods that I prayed to had punished me so badly for the ten cents collection! I felt I had lost my voice and my 'lawyer dream' forever.

I was in the Red Crescent Society. I remember we had to line up and count our numerical position in order. When my turn came up, I would pause. My heart would pump really fast. My face would feel hot and red under the hot sun. The student standing next to me would help and remind me of the number as though I did not know the order of numbers.

Answering phone calls was very difficult. Sometimes, even the word 'Hello' would not come out of my mouth. I struggled a lot but tried to be brave by adding words like 'ah, ah' to continue talking. Sometimes, I would let my siblings pick up the phone if I had a choice.

There was a senior boy who was one of the top three in my school. His dad was a school headmaster and my dad was a teacher in his school. My dad would proudly talk about the senior boy. I remember him going around my classes, popping up wherever I was and I could sense he was falling in love with me. However, falling in love was like a taboo in my time and in my family. Dad would have disowned me if I had done so. The boy moved to city school to do his A Levels. One day his school Tamil club organised a quiz. So, again, I had pressure from my school Tamil club to enter the quiz competition. "It will be really difficult," I thought! The very challenging task would be my blocked speech and moreover he was my secret crush. It was a real challenge. I thought, "How am I going to impress my sweetheart!"

He was the host and he asked a question and my answer would not come out of my mouth. It was the greatest embarrassing moment in my life as I could not impress him. I went back home and was quiet all day and felt sad that my blocked speech was obstructing my own feeling of development.

Why is life so difficult for me? Where were my words and why did they stick and why are they not coming out? I thought I may have nerve problems in my brain!

FIGHTING BACK

That's when I decided to fight back at my blocked speech. I knew that the only way to reap my reward was through education. Therefore, I studied hard, doing at least an additional four hours at home on school days, working till 1.00 a.m. I felt really confident each time I scored top marks in my subjects, especially maths and chemistry.

I used to sing this hymn like a mantra in my heart. It was written by a South Indian poet, Bharatiyar. It says 'No fear, no fear even if the sky fall down on your head'. I would sing this in my heart while walking to school, to be fearless in communication. That's how I used to start my day each and every morning.

Dad had entered me into the 'tevaram' Hindu song competition at district level since I was twelve years old. I thought it would be a good technique to get rid of my stammer because the songs are sung for Hindu deities, the god would hear my voice and help me to find it. But how wrong I was at that age. I learnt over the years that there is actually no magic formula to cure stammering. In my early twenties, though, the experience of singing in big crowds within my community improved my confidence level. In fact, singing any kind of good song is a useful medium to express feelings, and will help anyone to feel the joy within themselves. The flow of a song can help a stammerer to sing fluently as long they are enjoying singing lyrics that they like.

The one thing that I was grateful for was that my dad would take us to the library on Fridays. I usually ended up standing in the adventure story books corner, particularly those written by Enid Blyton. I was so obsessed with reading; trekking and camping stories mainly. Dad also subscribed to Reader's Digest magazine. I read those real life adventure stories. He never liked me to socialise, especially with boys, simply because my sister married at a young age and he did not want to lose another young daughter. I usually spent my school holidays reading Reader's Digest so that I could improve my English. I learnt English mostly by myself. During the school holidays, Dad encouraged me to look for five difficult words every day and write sentences using them and he would mark them. That's how I learnt English.

JUNGLE TREKKING

In 1991, my Additional Maths teacher organised a jungle trek at Taman Negara National Park. This is where the highest mountain in Peninsula Malaysia and the second highest in Malaysia stands. The land of Taman Negara National Park is more than 130 million years old and boasts the oldest tropical rainforest in the world. I was really excited telling my parents about it. My younger brother also wanted to join this expedition as his classmates joined the expedition too. However, my parents could only afford MYR 75.00 for one of us. As I was near to completing Form 5 in that school, my mum and dad agreed for me to join the trek thinking my brother would have a chance of trekking in the near future. He was very disappointed.

My mum worked in Singapore and took me there for shopping. I bought my first backpack there. I packed my clothes and the food listed by my schoolteachers.

I was really excited to step into my dream world in reality. I realised that I was the only Indian girl on that school trip.

My trekking group, teachers and I headed to Johore Bahru train station to take the night train to Jerantut, Pahang. We reached Jerantut in the morning. We were picked up to go to Kuala Tembeling Jetty. There were restaurants near the jetty. We had our breakfast before taking a boat to Kuala Tahan Jetty.

It was a three hour boat ride. The river water was clean but muddy coloured. Along the way, I saw very tall trees with lianas. It amazed me to see the lianas tangling around trees. Bamboos could be found. I saw aborigines washing their clothes near the river bank. Their kids were swimming alongside the river bank and waved at us. I saw a group of buffaloes soaking in the river water too and tiny birds flying around. The water flow and current can be fast sometimes. The boat driver had to slow down and ride as safely as possible.

After three hours of boat ride, we finally reached Kuala Tahan Jetty. We climbed up steep and short steps to the Park Ranger's office. Our teachers sorted out permits and camping arrangements for us.

Two big tents were pitched – one for girls and one for boys – at the allocated campsite. There were shower rooms and toilets a few yards away from the campsite.

We were in a group. We were briefed about not screaming, staying safe, staying in a group or informing the other team members if we were going somewhere else. I went to take a shower before making dinner. Some of the other group members had already started their cooking.

After enjoying my shower for the day, upon approaching my campsite, I saw my other team members were looking very worried and anxious. I saw a male and a female student lying on the fly sheet with red burnt skin. They were given first aid treatment. I heard from others that there had been plastic bags next to them when they were cooking their dinner and the bags were set on fire by a portable Bunsen burner. The students were in real pain.

Then, the female student went to lie in the girls' tent. I went inside to look for her and fan her leg to cool down the burning sensation.

I thought, "It is our first day, and it looks like they are not going to come with us for the trekking on the following days as they have to rest and are wounded quite badly."

We cooked our meal and made sure no plastic bags were near the portable Bunsen burner. That was the first vital lesson I learnt about camping. I slept in our tent. I used my backpack as my pillow and slept without a mat. I thought in my mind, "I have to sacrifice my comfortable bed just to see and feel the camping experience which I have been dreaming of for eight years."

The following day was a fine and dry one. We trekked using the jungle trail to Bukit Teresek, which is about 1.7 kilometres from the Park Ranger's office. I could hear the orchestra of forest insect noise along the trail. I was fascinated to see lush green everywhere. Trees were thin and tall, but provided good shade. We were trekking in one line. I had to learn how to balance my walking on the jungle trail – sometimes walking over tree roots and holding tree stems to find balance. We reached Bukit Teresek; at 334 metres it was the first hill in my life at the age of 18. I was thrilled as I caught a glimpse of Gunung Tahan – the highest mountain in Peninsula Malaysia.

We also explored Gua Telinga (Ear Cave, as the formation of the limestone cave looks like a human ear). We were advised to wear a long sleeved t-shirt, long trousers and a cap and to take a torch with us. I explored inside; it was dark and damp and smelled of bats' droppings. I saw bats on the cave wall and they started to fly and I felt the wind. "We must have frightened them," I thought.

Along the jungle trail, we spotted a Rafflesia flower (the world's largest flower). I could see flies around it and it stank. But we were lucky to see that flower in Taman Negara.

We rested at one resting area. Suddenly, I saw a few leeches sucking blood on my legs. I was screaming. My friend pulled the fat leeches away. I hate leeches and all sorts of thought went through my mind...what if it happened to enter...it was so scary even to think about it!

The next plan was to trek to Yong Hide. It's like a hut on a tree and is the best way to observe wild animals. It was raining and so we wore ponchos. The trail along the terrain was slippery and I slipped. Thank God, a fellow trekker grabbed my hand, otherwise I would have fallen into the river next to the terrain. We finally reached the hide. There were steps to go up to the hide. There were bunk beds without mattresses. We shared our hide with a foreign couple. This was where we had the chance to see wildlife. We sat on the bench so quietly to observe animals like deer or wild boar, but, unfortunately, I only saw a butterfly. That was funny!

It was time to complete our camping activities. The jungle trekking, camping, caving, walking on terrain in Taman Negara were the most fulfilling activities I had ever experienced in my life. That was my first exposure to nature. We left Kuala Tahan Jetty by boat to Kuala Tembeling Jetty. When I got into the boat, I turned back to the dense rainforest and promised to return to the same forest, but the next time would be to climb Mount Tahan (Gunung Tahan) – the second highest in Malaysia.

FURTHER EDUCATION

I realised that my confidence had risen among my classmates; in fact I studied even harder to get the best marks in my maths and science subjects.

After I had completed my Form 5 exams, my dad wanted me to pursue A Levels in a private college that offers a twinning programme to do a university degree in Australia.

My heart and mind were not into doing a degree in a foreign country. It was simply because Mum and Dad already struggled financially. Mum worked so hard. She worked in the afternoon and night time in Singapore. Sometimes, I hardly saw her during weekdays. I started to miss her and would do all the house chores so that she could rest at home.

My dad made an appointment with a course advisor and I went along with heavy heart. I was not interested in their conversation at all. Dad could sense that. We came back home. I said, "I am not going to Australia. I just want to go to the University of Malaya." Dad raised his voice and told Mum, "Tell your daughter that I am not digging a grave for her. I am doing the best for her own future. That's it!"

I was so sad and, for the first time, I slammed the door in front of my parents. I threw myself on my bed and cried, "Dad, you do not realise what impact you have had on me and you made me the person who I am now."

I passed my Form 5 exams and was one of the top ten students in the school. I was admitted to do science subjects in Form 6, which is equivalent to A Level. Somehow, my friend's brother advised me to change to Arts subjects; he said I would have more chance of passing A Level exams and would have a better chance of going to university as we had a quota system for Muslim and Non-Muslim. Since the age of ten, I had always wanted to go to the University of Malaya as it was the most prestigious university in Malaysia at that time. It was not easy to change to another class. I wasted nearly six months in science class before being accepted into the Arts class. I really worked hard to catch up with other students in Arts. This is when I was exposed to making presentations.

Covert Stammerer

I would write my presentation notes by choosing the short words that I could easily say without stammering. I did not have any therapy. My parents did not know anything about my stammer. The school did not have any system to support someone like me. No one knew that I was suffering emotionally inside. That was my coping mechanism to overcome my stammer.

I attended a motivational seminar in Muar, Johore. I participated in 'soul searching' activity. It was about 'you and your ultimate goal in your life'. It was a sort of meditation programme, visualising oneself to attain one's goal. I practised that for many years, so before going to do any climb, I would picture myself standing on the summit.

I passed my A Level exams and was the best in my school. I applied to the University of Malaya and got admitted to do Economics subjects. My parents did not have enough money to fund my university studies. I thought one day, "Thank God I did not go to Australia." My eldest brother funded my first semester fee and I took two university loans to fund my four years of study. I wanted to do Accountancy in Year 2 but I did not achieve good results. Therefore, I ended up doing Business Administration papers from Year 2 until my final year. In addition to that, I studied Mandarin. I thought I would have a better chance to get a good job by having an extra language. I passed the first year paper, failed second year and repeated in third year. The classes usually took place in late afternoon. I remembered my university friends would be socialising in the evenings but I would be attending extra classes. Somehow, I enjoyed the friends I had in the Chinese class. Some of them were university professors and well known people. I remember one of my best birthday gifts was when a Chinese classmate's little daughter played the 'Happy Birthday' tune on the piano on my birthday. I simply felt so much appreciated in life as others always admired my courage in choosing to learn the Mandarin language.

I could easily befriend people, especially easily conversing one to one with confidence; but not speaking publicly, because of stage fright.

PRESENTATION

One of the university requirements to complete a degree course was submission of a project paper or thesis and presentation to the lecturer and to classmates. I loved writing project papers and doing research and I was really great at it simply because I could write up the evidence I had collected. There is no restriction on creativity and imagination in my mind. The title was 'Consumers' Perception towards Insurance'. I chose this title feeling that my successful work experience would allow me to produce a final year paper. I employed a quality writing skill on the project paper and I had two lecturers to support me. I researched to find good presentation techniques and felt that visual aids would enhance my presentation skills. So, I bought a wooden house from an art and craft shop. I got the shopkeeper to paint on the wooden house words that describe the necessity of having life insurance. I wrote my presentation notes carefully using words that I could say and that would not block my speech.

I always had financial problems. My parents only had enough money to support university funding for one child and at that time my younger brother's university fee was higher than mine. Finance is always an issue in my family. Mum set up a food business. She funded my younger brother's university studies from the profit.

I did not have money to buy a suit for the presentation. A friend of mine was kind enough to lend me her blouse and two piece skirt suit. It was green and I felt so confident wearing a suit, to be honest. The second lecturer was actually from my Mandarin class, whom I had met in 1997. I did the best ever presentation in my life. I gained an 'A' for the project paper and that meant my papers would be displayed in the University of Malaya's library for the next few decades at least. I was so proud of myself for the achievement as one day I would be able to show the hardback project to my future children.

I realised that if I had my own creative visual aids and someone I was comfortable with to present to, I could have great presentation skills.

CLIMBING

At the beginning of 1997, my dad reminded me about my mountain climbing aspirations as I had said to him one day that I would climb Mount Kinabalu, the highest mountain in Malaysia, before completing my degree course. So, I decided to enquire about a mountain climbing expedition. I had a few friends from Sabah, so I decided to join Sabah's Student Association's annual climbing programme. I did not do much training. In fact the training was just a couple of times running around the house. That's all.

I sponsored my younger brother to join the expedition.

I was so passionate to help Indian students who came from a poor family background or were struggling in education.

In the same year, I organised a major event for Indian students from my former secondary school with the help of my brother's friends. They were mainly undergraduates like me. I had meetings with the schoolteachers, lecturer, doctor, army personnel, spoke to various organisations, raised sponsorships to run the motivational programme. However, the saddest story was that I chose not to be head of the programme but to run and co-ordinate the programme, because I knew I would not be able to stand in front of a crowd to give the opening and closing speeches. I tried to avoid giving public speeches as much as possible.

In May 1997, my brother and I flew to Sabah and that was the first time I took a plane. We joined the University of Malaya Sabah's Association group.

My younger brother climbed really well whereas I was one of the slowest ones. I had blisters on my feet and it was a horrible experience; however, I enjoyed the beauty of the nature.

It was freezing cold at Laban Rata, where most climbers rest for the night. I went to lie down in my warmed-up bed. I put the TV on. What I watched refuelled my motivation to climb to the summit. It was about Malaysian climbers scaling Mount Everest. Their climb was broadcast on television and I was thrilled. I thought I would have been in that group if I had known there was such an expedition! My passion grew even stronger to climb Mount Everest.

On 13.5.1997 I first summited Low's Peak, Mount Kinabalu (4101 metres) in Sabah – the highest summit in South East Asia. I found the climb really challenging as I had not trained much. I was one of the last ones in the group to complete the climb.

On 23.5.1997 Datuk Magendran reached the summit of Everest followed by Mohandas 15 minutes later. They were the first Malaysians to step onto Mount Everest. I was so genuinely proud of them and wanted to meet them personally and tell them my dream. But it was not an easy task to approach public figures like them.

They were going around the country giving talks about their successful expedition. At that time I was working part time as an insurance agent to add to my pocket money. I decided to take a flight from Kuala Lumpur to Johore Bahru in the hope of meeting them at an airport. That was the first time in my life I ran around after someone in order to strike up a conversation to make my dream come true. I would be looking around for crowds.

Somehow, I never did see them anywhere at the airport. Meanwhile, I was becoming popular in my university for climbing Mount Kinabalu during my final year. I had juniors around admiring me all the time.

I would usually attend a Hindu religious talk on Fridays. One day, on the way back from the talk, I walked past the university restaurant and my juniors called me. I turned and walked towards them. Whom did I see? Wow! It was Datuk Magendran – the Malaysian Everest climber.

He had been accepted at the University of Malaya to do a sports science degree course. I was so nervous that I forgot my own name for a few seconds. Before I introduced myself, my juniors had already mentioned me. He asked me whether I could be a coach for the lady climbers and my answer was "Yes" straight away without thinking for a second…So, that's how I developed my climbing a bit further. I joined his residential college team for training. The training was quite hard and demanding. I was doing extra running in the morning on the weekends.

I had seen Magendran's Mount Everest slide presentation. That was the first time I realised that I might do the Mount Everest climb, but not a presentation because of my blocked speech. I was not confident at all to give such a presentation to the media or the public. I still had the fear of communication. I felt stammering was still the part of me that stopped me from socialising and the reason for an unaccountable feeling of isolation.

In October 1997, I coached the girls and climbed Mount Kinabalu for the second time in the same year. Air Asia sponsored our flight tickets. My dad contributed MYR 500.00, which was quite a lot of money at that time. The climb attracted wide media publicity. The expedition was filmed as a documentary.

I remember one of the girls who found climbing Kinabalu really tough. As a coach I told her to make her own decision whether she wanted to summit the next day. It was a hard decision to make as she was physically exhausted. She made her decision to climb and so I stayed with her. I had the privilege to climb with Magendran at the same time with her. He was a hero to everyone. Somehow, although the girl was suffering she managed to climb but it was too hard to scale down. I heard from others someone carried her to the foot of the mountain. That's when I realised how decision making was so crucial, especially in mountaineering when you take risk into consideration.

I did not feel any pain after the climb due to my intensive training. Each expedition taught me valuable lessons; this one particularly on training, risk taking, decision making and time keeping as we had to start trekking up to the summit around 1.30 a.m. so that we could be at the summit by 5.30 a.m., otherwise it would be dangerous up there on the top.

I realised that my self confidence was getting stronger after two climbs in the same year. It was simply because of my brand as a mountain climber among my university friends.

My dad and I usually wrote letters to each other and as my fame grew in my final year because of climbing, I asked him why was I born into this world. His reply in his letter was the most shocking news of my life because he finally disclosed to me that my mum conceived me while he was in his mental illness state. I could not swallow that news at all. I wondered what my mother would have been thinking of while I was in her womb. I could not believe this at all as he was leading a normal life as everyone else. Not only that, my family lived near Jerantut at that time and he told me that one day he cycled to Kuala Tembeling Jetty…From that moment, somehow, I felt like there was a strong connection between me and Taman Negara, Pahang…

23

MY DAD'S MENTAL ILLNESS

At age six dad realised that his walking was slightly different from his peers' and he asked his mother why. His mum said that when he was about one year old she had left him on a mat with an older girl outside their house for a little while. The girl carried him but he slipped from her and fell. He cried instantly. His mum hurried to see and he was on the floor. His leg swelled so much. She took him to doctors but at that time it was very difficult to reach good medical treatment. As a result, he limped when he started to walk.

I always wondered and wanted to know what could have caused his mental illness. My dad was a truthful, very disciplined and structured man. He planned his day in the morning, the things he wanted to do. He was very ambitious. However, his disability had delayed his progress in many aspects of his life. He was a very hard working man. He read a lot. He highly talked about George Bernard Shaw, Mahatma Gandhi, Winston Churchill and Abraham Lincoln. He loved to draw and he drew portraits of them on his drawing art blocks. When I was little I admired his art skills.

He also lived in an era of British, Japanese and Communists for the first seventeen years of his life. A few of his uncles on his mother's side supported him when he was a child and a teenager. One uncle even bought for him a bicycle so that he could go to his night classes as there was no public transport to his night school.

When he became a qualified teacher in January 1967, he wanted to marry his uncle's daughter but his uncle refused his proposal by saying my dad's astrological sign did not match with his daughter's. He was upset and told his mum too. He did not believe that the signs did not match so he approached an astrologer in the Carmen estate, who said Dad's and his sweetheart's astrology signs did match. He was extremely upset and could not sleep nearly for two weeks and he wanted to go back to his hometown. More

Mahatma Gandhi portrait drawn by my Dad

over, this request was declined by the school headmaster. He was extremely disappointed. One evening, he packed his bag and took a taxi to Kuala Lumpur. The taxi driver was a Chinese. He arrived at Kuala Lumpur and he did not know what to do. He realised that his mind was affected very badly by not sleeping for two weeks. He was worried that he was going to be mentally ill. He spent his night in the taxi. He got down from the taxi. He did not have any money in his hand. Next to the taxi station was a coffee shop. He went upstairs to the coffee shop looking for a place to sleep.

Suddenly, he felt a Chinese worker from the coffee shop following closely behind him and hit the back of his head. He was bleeding and his shirt was covered with blood. My dad was very angry and attacked him back. My dad was unconscious after that. People gathered and the taxi driver took my dad away and left him at a police station. My dad opened his eyes and realised he was at a police station. After a short discussion with a police officer, my dad was sent to Kuala Lumpur General Hospital. At the hospital, Dad was accompanied by a police officer. The officer thought my dad was about to attack him and pointed a gun at him. My dad was angry and said, "Shoot my chest if you want to!" Dad was immediately sent to the prisoner's ward, where he was imprisoned. He spent his sleepless nights in a cell. There was a Sikh prisoner next to his cell. The prisoner recalled that my dad was talking unconsciously about world leaders' powerful quotations! He kept drawing his dad's face and said his uncle's name countless times. He was given food and a doctor came to inject him. He could not remember anything or any events after that for many nights. He regained consciousness and found he had been placed at Tanjung Rambutan Mental Hospital in Ipoh, Perak. His mum and his relatives visited after he became conscious. His mum kissed him to comfort him. They took him back to Permas estate –to his home village. That was how 1967 ended for him! It was the beginning of a teaching career but also the start of mental illness!

His medication made him feel drowsy and sleepy all the time. His youngest brother cared for him after school hours. In 1968 he had psychotic episodes and was admitted to a mental hospital for two weeks. His relatives started to look at and react very differently to him after his mental illness. Nevertheless, my dad worked really hard and was committed to his teaching professionalism.

He married my mum on 13.12.1969. My mum dedicated her entire life to my dad to ensure he led a normal life. Mum always told us Dad would experience an episode if he missed his sleep. So, as children we did not spend much time with Dad. Dad can get angry sometimes and as a result he would shout at us very badly. We would not even talk openly in our family. As siblings, we grew up our own way! That's why until now no one in my family knew about my blocked speech. My elder brother stammers very badly. My dad did not have the patience to support my elder brother with his speech when he was a child and over the years he developed severe speech impairment.

MORE CLIMBS

To my mind, I needed solid climbing experience before going to Mount Everest. So, after the successful second Kinabalu expedition, I was planning to do Mount Korbu (2183 metres) in Ipoh, which is the second highest mountain in Peninsula Malaysia. Mount Korbu is one of the more difficult mountains to climb in Malaysia and there had already been incidents of death.

I used to practise my Mandarin language with selected Chinese university mates. One of them was Annie Low Ean Nee – a mature student, my junior. I told her that I wanted to organise Mount Korbu in March 2008. She then introduced me to a mountain ranger and also a climber who was a postman from Ipoh, Perak. His name was Mr Chong Sing Woh. He had experience of taking climbers to Mount Korbu and Annie had been in his climb, where he was the ranger.

Mount Ledang

I organised and led the Mount Ledang (1276 metres) expedition in December 1997 as part of the preparation for Mount Korbu and eventually Everest. This was my first role as a leader. I led a team of ten climbers. I phoned the Ledang office to organise the expedition.

I realised that I was not troubled by blocked speech in my phone conversations any more simply because I was very excited and happy with what I was doing and there was no fear in expressing my joy of climbs. Also, I realised I was not stammering when I was the first one to talk rather than waiting for my turn to talk, like in class, when it made me very anxious with racing heartbeat.

Climbing Mount Ledang is quite challenging. One has to be physically fit for this one. We were blessed with fine and dry weather. We summited Mount Ledang on 26.12.1997. I prayed in my heart on the summit to get a blessing for my Mount Everest expedition.

Mount Korbu

I contacted Mr Chong Sing Woh on the phone and agreed to meet him at Ipoh to discuss further about Mount Korbu before the actual climb.

I saw Mr Chong at Ipoh bus station. He looked so fit and smiled to see me. I was happy to see him and made sure that I looked confident during our discussion. Mr Chong could not be our ranger but kindly arranged for us a native guide who lived in the foothills of Korbu.

Mr Chong alerted me that Mount Korbu was a tough one to climb and had its own challenges to throw at us. He said it was most important to follow the guide, respect the mountain, no screaming or shouting, especially no chopping trees or breaking branches, and, more importantly to ask permission of the mountain lord to answer calls of nature. The mountains are regarded as lords by the aboriginals! "This is another valuable lesson to learn," I thought.

I had to brief my team on what Mr Chong warned about not respecting Mount Korbu, even in our thoughts! That was a very strong message. This is because two young climbers died of gas poisoning on the summit the previous year. One of them was Rohan Nair, an experienced mountaineer! It was a tragedy! In fact, Mr Chong was one of the rangers for that team.

So, as a leader of this expedition I had a huge responsibility for my own life and other climbers' lives! I had to ensure the climbers were physically fit and they actually were climbing to fulfil their purpose.

I had to make sure the climbers packed only necessary items that were as light as possible to carry to avoid physical exhaustion. Magendran was very kind and lent his tent and stove and wished us well for the expedition.

We reached Ipoh on 22.03.1998. It took a while to get police clearance. The next day we met our native guide. He was only wearing an old t-shirt, shorts and rubber shoes. He was very quiet but he guided us safely. We always stayed together as a group as this was dense forest and the trails were narrow. We religiously prayed to this mountain at the beginning and ending of each camp.

We reached the impressive and beautiful summit on 24.03.1998. I had a unique experience on this summit. It was very windy that night and none of us could sleep well in our tents because of the howling noise of the wind. We told this to our native guide. He sang a song in his native language and all of a sudden the wind slowed down and was calm. It was a sort of unseen power whom he talked to. I personally felt that this was an auspicious mountain and I will never forget that moment!

We were the only group climbing the mountain around that date range.

We climbed down the next day. It was quite tiring and we were exhausted by the time we reached the foothills late at night. What

1998- Mt Korbu foot mountain, the first from the right was the native guide

1997-Mt Ledang summit, I was standing on the first left, my youngest brother Elanggoh, standing second from the right

2001- One of the many mini gardens on Mt Bintang

2002- Rope climbing on Mt Ledang, Uncle Yap was ahead of me

2002-Mt Tahan expedition mates. Sitting from right- Groover Wan, me, Ms Ng. Standing from right- Bala, Mr Chong, Chee Hong, Wee Mian, Uncle Chong and Mr Yap

2002- On Mt Tahan trail, looking for the summit

2002- On Mt Tahan- attractive quartz crystals scattered near summit slope

May 2016 -Kevinathan and Reganathan on a walk on Snowdon

a surprise – Mr Chong waited for us on his bike! He brought Chinese noodles for us and they tasted so delicious. We all deserved the food after the treacherous climb.

What I learnt from this expedition was climbing is not about competition. It is about working as a team to reach our destination. We needed each other to support ourselves.

Ever since then, I have kept in touch with Mr Chong, who has been the greatest supporter in my climbing life to date. I was always delighted to get letters from him. I asked him one day what he had thought of me when he first saw me. His answer was, he'd thought I was "...a keen mountaineer and a leader with clear direction in your mind!"

RISE ABOVE FAILURE

During the Mount Korbu expedition, one of the climbers fell in love with me. When I returned home, he started to make contact and I decided to develop my first love with this man. Somehow, due to the long distance between us, the friendship did not last long; he decided to break it off. As with everyone, first love was special. I could not take the rejection from him straight away and it took couple of years for me to accept it. I wished I could be more expressive through my communication and blamed my stammer for not being myself.

In Malaysia, back in 1998, it was so difficult to get a job. My dad retired and he offered me his teaching role to take on as a last resort if I did not get a job within a month. I knew my clock was ticking. I applied for hundreds of jobs, went for interviews; the interviewers would turn me down saying, "You have no related work experience". Once, I got really furious with the interviewer. I asked her back, "Who is going to give me work experience if not employers like yourself?" She answered, "I can keep your CV on file." I replied, "No, if you cannot give me a job now, you are not going to give me a job in the future." I was really disappointed as I had worked so hard, studied day and night, plus learning an extra language at university. Most of my university mates ended up studying further in teaching positions due to a lack of graduate teachers in Malaysia. I thought to myself, "Being a teacher will be the hardest job in my life as I have to deal every day with my fear of communication."

The thirty day period my dad had given was over. I did not have any choice. I had to accept my dad's offer and become a temporary teacher of primary school children.

The following year, I managed to get a job in Singapore as Sales Admin Clerk. I worked in two different companies and left Singapore in 2001. My colleagues used to laugh as my Mandarin was not good enough, not like a fluent speaker. I felt so inferior sometimes. I felt life was difficult simply because I had a dream and I was not prepared to let it go.

Dad wanted to help me buy a house with his pension money. He said he would contribute towards the deposit as he wanted me to own a house. But, as my mind was in climbing, I said I did not want to and would not be able to keep up with mortgage payments as climbing is a really expensive hobby. So, he bought a house for my younger brother and, as he was studying, my dad put my name and my older brother's names as guarantors.

I managed to get another job in Ranbaxy as a medical rep. I worked for six months. This job required me to travel from Johore Bahru to Kuala Lumpur and covered a wide area of the southern part of Malaysia. I had to drive hundreds of miles to see doctors in remote areas to get orders for drugs. I truly embraced that I needed to be bold and brave to overcome my fear of communication and also being on my own to deal with challenging aspects of life. I made an effort to look confident in selling drugs and taking orders from doctors. Some of the medicine names are very difficult to pronounce and I tried so hard, practising saying medicine names such as 'Amoxicillin' while I was driving the car. I gained more confidence every time I gained sales orders. It meant I was able to talk to medical professionals, they understood my verbal communication and I convinced them to buy stocks from my company. It was the experience that I went for to boost my confidence. I enjoyed driving in remote areas and loved the beauty of nature. But I got tired driving and wanted to settle down, I thought. I applied for a teaching position but this time as temporary secondary school teacher.

Warren Macdonald

In 2000, I read a story in Reader's Digest magazine about Warren Macdonald, who lost his legs in April 1997 during a rock fall on a Mount Bowen climb in Australia. Nevertheless, he never stopped climbing!

I asked my office colleague to purchase his book, One Step Beyond, online. Warren sent the book with a handwritten note, "To pass to him". He thought I was a bloke. I laughed when I saw the note. Perhaps he did not realise an Indian woman could be a climber too.

He is the second public figure whom I made contact with. He had a deep respect for nature and animals. His story inspired me. He has the courage, strength and power to move on and willingness to lead others. He would reply to my e-mails no matter how busy he was, and he inspired me by how much he can do as a human to inspire other humans with his physical limitations. He found no excuse not to reply my e-mails, me a complete stranger. He is amazing!

FURTHER CLIMBS

I joined Perak's Recreation Club. They actively organised climbing expeditions. This is when Mr Chong introduced me to Mr Ismail, Uncle Chong, Mr Bala, Uncle Yap and Groover Wan. They are my backbones, they believed in me and they gave a life towards my dream. Mr Bala worked at Tanjung Rambutan Mental Hospital. Once, Mr Chong took me to see him. When I went to the hospital I saw a few patients and I thought of my dad, thinking he would have gone through the same sort of experience in a mental ward.

So, my climbing continued again in March 2001 when I summited Mount Bintang (1862 metres). Then, in October 2001–Mount Angsi (825 m), December 2001 – Mount Pulai (654 m), February 2002 – Mount Ledang (1276 m), April 2002 – Mount Suku (1797 m), May 2002 – Mount Tahan (2187 m), December 2002 – Mount Nuang (1493 m), July 2003 – Mount Ledang (1276 m) as part of the preparation for Mount Everest.

Mount Tahan (Mount of Endurance) was the pinnacle of my climbs and a very successful one. I was the leader. It took a year for me to plan, organise and train for this climb.

Mount Tahan Challenge (25.5.2002 to 1.6.2002)

Mount Tahan is situated in Taman Negara National Park, which holds the oldest tropical jungle in the world.

The first expedition to Mount Tahan was carried out by the Chief Minister of Pahang, Bendahara Ahmad. The aim of the expedition was not stated but it is very likely that Bendahara Ahmad was looking for gold due to the state's financial situation. Pahang's output of gold was well known as far away as Australia. The traditional folklore tells us that the mountain's rivers could have been a good source of gold. Bendahara Ahmad's attempt was not successful though, because the route was not clear enough.

Europeans also made attempts to climb this mountain. Despite failures, many carried out the same expedition. The successful one was made by HC Robinson with four other Malay helpers on 16.7.1905. He was the curator of the Selangor State Museum.

The expedition revealed that there was no gold on Mount Tahan but one could see attractive quartz crystals scattered on the summit slopes glittering in the sunlight. These crystals could have been the real source of Mount Tahan's legend.

1st Day: Kuala Tahan to Melantai Campsite

The team consisted of Uncle Chong, Mr Yap, Mr Chong, Mr Bala, Groover, Chee Hong, Wee Mian, Mr Ku and Ms Ng.

We were at the Ranger's Office before 8 a.m. to declare our goods and belongings. It took about 40 minutes. Mr Fuad, the ranger, arrived at 9.00 a.m. At 9.10 a.m., after a short prayer, we started our six day adventure of the Mount Tahan challenge.

Climbing Mount Tahan was my eleven-year dream and I understood that some other climbers too had the same dream as mine. When I started to trek, I saw huge trees around me. They provided good shade for us. There were lots of small plants with big leaves and tiny flowers. The trail was flat and damp due to rain earlier in the day. Most of the time, we had to jump over tree trunks that had fallen on the trail. After some distance, there was a turn-off for the main trail to Mount Tahan 55 kilometres to the summit. As we walked through the forest I was extremely happy to finally make my eleven years of dreaming come true. We had to cross small streams as well and our shoes got wet too.

One needs to have a good pair of shoes or boots for any climbing but I noticed my newly bought boot's sole had come apart. I told Mr Chong and Mr Yap about it. Mr Yap is a very practical climber. He used a piece of string to tie up the torn part of the sole to my boot. In fact, that morning a boat driver had warned that my boots were not the right ones for this mountain!

"How am I going to climb my dream mountain with these boots for the next six days?" I wondered. "And all this has happened even before reaching Melantai itself!" I thought. Our tentative plan for the first day was to trek to Kem Tengah. Just then, we met two native porters with a schoolteacher and a school student. The student was injured and the two porters were taking them to the foothills but they, the porters, needed to return to Melantai Campsite to rejoin their group. Mr Chong had a brilliant idea and asked them to buy two pairs of rubber shoes for me, the type mainly used by natives.

After six hours of trekking, we reached Melantai campsite at 3.25 p.m. The altitude was about 100 metres (300 feet). There was a small stream. What surprised us was a swarm of bees that surrounded us, our climbing equipment and haversacks. Many of us got stung. After pitching our tents, we washed ourselves in the river to get rid of the sticking smell of sweat. But the bees, I guess, considered us as flowers, looking for honey perhaps!

We cooked dinner, discussed with Mr Fuad about the next day's plan. We rested in our tents.

Finally that night, the two natives returned to our campsite and passed me the rubber shoes. I kept a pair and then gave them the second pair as a gift, as suggested by Mr Chong. Even though it only cost me MYR 4.00 the real value was more like MYR 400.00. To me the native porters were my God-sent messengers. My worries vanished from my mind and I drifted into a deep sleep in the middle of thick jungle in my tent under a starry sky.

2nd Day: Melantai Campsite to Kuala Puteh

On the second day, we had to cross 27 hills on the ridge.

Our plan was to continue trekking at 5.30 a.m. but since some of our torches were not functioning very well, it was already 6.45 a.m. by the time we dismantled our tents and cleared the campsite.

We had to cross a stream and started the day's steep climb at 250 metres. We reached Kem Tengah at 11.50 a.m. and had our lunch there. We then headed to Kuala Puteh. At 1.15 p.m. we reached Gunung Rajah at 576 metres, which is the highest hill on the ridge. The view was very clear but the swarm of bees did not let us to stay long on the summit.

We then descended all the way down to Kuala Puteh. It started to pour heavily even before we reached Kuala Puteh. We trekked in the rain and reached Kuala Puteh at 4 p.m. My team mates spread a flysheet and we rested underneath it. I shared my chocolate and oat biscuits with my team mates and they tasted heavenly at that time.

We noticed leeches sticking on our legs. I had to pull them off from my skin. I hate leeches and it was one of my nightmares whenever I was in damp thick forest.

The rain finally stopped around 5.30 p.m. Mr Yap always loved cooking during our mountain climbs so he cooked dinner for us. When the rain stopped, we were surrounded by bees again. The bees were another challenge to us. In reality, Kuala Puteh is a very beautiful campsite.

3rd Day: Kuala Puteh to Kuala Teku to Wray's Camp

The best part was that all of us stayed close and so no one got left behind. We began our trekking at 7.10 a.m. We entered a dense forest, and the trail led to the banks of a river. The bamboos along the river bank were so beautiful in the morning sunlight. We had to walk along a very narrow and slippery bank before crossing the river. I spotted beautiful big, white and pink flowers fallen on the trails and they gave off a mild fragrance. It was so enjoyable looking at the beautiful view while trekking.

We made the first river crossing at 9.00 a.m. It was a good idea to use a stick during a river crossing. Out of the six river crossings that we made, three rivers were very difficult to cross because of the strong current, having to walk on slippery and sharp rocks, as well as the high water level – as high as our waists. What was on all our minds was 'Kepala Air' (Water Head), which refers to the first and sudden water flow with a very strong current. The climbers were aware of this and we all crossed the rivers cautiously. There had been incidents resulting in severe injuries previously because of the Water Head during river crossings.

When I reached the last river crossing, I thanked God for His blessings and for providing us with good and fine weather.

We continued our trekking to Wray's Camp in our wet clothes and soaked socks and shoes. We had our lunch on our way up. It was a continual uphill climb. My calves hurt and my pace became slower and slower. I learnt from Uncle Chong to move on step by step at a slow and continuous pace. After every fifty steps, I rested a while. All of us were exhausted by the time we reached Wray's Camp. It was cold and misty, so we quickly changed into dry clothes. The campsite was quite narrow. There was a water source, but to get there one needed to descend on a slippery and narrow trail. The third day was an exhausting and tiring climb. It was really cold that night. My sleeping bag kept me warm but somehow I could not sleep well.

4th Day: Wray's Camp to Mount Gedong

The fourth day of our journey began. Our plan was to reach the summit of Mount Tahan today and camp there. According to our ranger, the sunrise and sunset on Mount Gedong's summit would be even clearer than on the Mount Tahan summit.

We left Wray's Camp (1100 metres) at 8.10 a.m. The distance from Wray's Camp to Mount Pankin (1463 metres) was two kilometres. We reached Mount Pankin at 10.30 a.m. There was no water source all along the way from Wray's Camp until we reached Mount Pankin. The water at Mount Pankin was tea coloured and we used sterilising tablets to purify it. The trail to the water source was muddy and very soft.

Soon after that, we headed to Mount Tangga 15 (1539 metres) and reached it at 12.10 noon. I wondered about such a funny name. It means 'fifteen stairs of mountain'. According to Mr Fuad, in the past, one had to go through fifteen bouts of rock climbing, up and down, using rope. But a shorter route with fewer rock climbs has been introduced. However, the original name has remained up to today.

After lunch, we continued uphill and downhill along the ridge. I was fascinated by the mesmerising sight of Mount Tangga 15. I must say that I had never seen such a beautiful sight on any other mountains that I had climbed before. I wondered if this was what is called a 'heavenly playground'. It was simply awesome, with a cold wind. I felt that the tiring journey was compensated for by those eye catching scenes. Twisted trees and white or light green mosses could be found everywhere on the rock.

At 3.10 p.m., after two and a half hours of trekking Mount Tangga 15, we reached Mount Resket (1666 metres). We rested a while and continued up to Mount Gedong (2066 metres). We had to climb uphill for 300 metres before reaching Mount Gedong. One needed to be careful here since some of the rocks were loose. So getting a strong grip before proceeding up is essential. Finally, we reached the pretty summit of Mount Gedong at 5.10 p.m.

It was quite windy with thick mist. Wild orchids, tiny monkey cups and mosses could be found here. Bonsai trees were only knee level. Quartz crystals could be seen everywhere on the trail. They glittered and shone. The picturesque mountain ranges added to our excitement even more. Padang Campsite could be seen very clearly from Mount Gedong summit. We pitched our tent and descended further down to collect drinking water.

The sunset captured our attention very much. I had my dinner while enjoying the sight of sunset. It was windy. After dinner, we discussed the next bid for the summit.

But something that angered me was that previous climbers had taken advantage of nature. Some had thrown sanitary pads and tissues. The pleasant view was marred by selfish climbers who did not appreciate nature's beauty.

5th Day: Summit Quest

As usual, Uncle Yap gave the 'wake up' call. I could hardly open my eyes. I did not want to miss the sunrise so I got up. The cloud hid the sun and the sunrise was not clear; only a layer of sunlight could be seen. But, a few minutes later, the clouds moved away and the sun emerged. I was overjoyed to see the sunrise. It was amazingly beautiful. It felt like "This is to the route to heaven". No words can describe the beauty of it. I felt so excited and felt energised with the power from the sun.

After breakfast, we dismantled our tents and at 7.35 a.m. we left for my dream summit.

There is a small valley between Mount Gedong and Mount Tahan. It was wet, muddy and slowed down our pace. Mosses, with wild species of orchids, pitcher plants and twisted trees could be found here too.

The final ascent was a steady climb of 350 metres to the summit. White patches of quartzite rock on the trail to the summit showed very clearly before we reached the summit. My group decided to put me as the first summitter and Ms Ng as the second, as this was her first mountain climb, followed by eight other climbers. At exactly 1.10 p.m. I stepped onto Mount Tahan's summit. I felt great joy after conquering the Mount Tahan summit. We carried a banner and snapped photos. We truly were extremely happy when we signed the banner. We had trekked fifty-five kilometres to reach the highest peak of Peninsula Malaysia in four and a half days.

On the other hand, the summit was not as impressive as other mountain summits I had climbed before. It was literally 'bald'. We had a short lunch there and we started to talk about the next trip to Mount Tahan. I told them I might return with my children one day. Uncle Chong said, "Perhaps my grandchildren will join you and my spirit will be with you." I said, "That will be great!" Now, our mission to scale Mount Tahan was complete and we descended after an hour.

While descending, the picturesque mountain range caught my eyes. I would say that each mountain has its own beauty and uniqueness.

We descended for two kilometres on a rock face trail to Botak Hills (1943 metres). We collected enough water for one day and left at 4 p.m. We reached Bonzai campsite at 5 p.m. and decided to camp for the night. It started to drizzle and then poured heavily. I collected the rainwater to clean myself. I had not had a shower for four days!

Soon after the rain stopped, Uncle Yap prepared dinner for us. While admiring twisted and bonsaid trees around us, we took our dinner. That night, I slept deeply.

Final Day: Bonzai Campsite to Kuala Juram (25.5 kilometres)

We descended at 7 a.m. and I really wondered if the group would complete the 25.5 kilometre descent on the final day. I told myself not to push anyone's limit but everyone trekked really fast. We reached Belumut campsite (1493 metres) at 9.30 a.m. We continued to Kubang (1406 m), the distance from Belumut to Kubang being 1.5 km. It was muddy and slippery. Orchids and mosses could be found here too. We reached Kubang at 10.20 a.m. and there was a water source there. We headed to Permatang at a distance of 3.5 km. The trees were thin and the trail was dry. After lunch we descended to Kem Kor (750 m) in 2.5 km and headed to Lata Luis (558 m) at 2.0 km. Lata Luis means Luis Waterfall. I cleaned my shoes, legs, arms and face. The water was cold and the refreshing air re-energised us to go ahead to the following campsite. Bees swarmed us again. We trekked 6 km down to Kuala Luis (306 m). Then, from Kuala Luis to Kuala Juram was another 5 km. We crossed small streams before reaching Kuala Juram and it poured heavily before we reached our last destination of the day. My heart jumped with happiness when I saw the bridge to Kuala Juram campsite at 5.55 p.m.

Our mission to challenge ourselves to climb Mount Tahan was completed on 31.5.2002. That night, we shared and cheered our success. Uncle Chong at age 72 was the second oldest to climb Mount Tahan. I was really proud of him to have made it at this age. I thanked my team for trusting my leadership and for their contribution to the success of this challenge.

Courage, determination, team spirit, physical fitness and mental endurance are the key needs in conquering this beautiful and awesome mountain. Most importantly, respect for nature, teamwork, trust, decision making and blessings from the mountains are key ingredients of a successful expedition. Experiencing them provides unforgettable memories that will last throughout the lives of climbers.

EVEREST DREAM

I was still keeping in touch with 'Everest Magendran' by telephone and letter. I was getting really depressed. I could strongly sense from my conversation with him that there was no sign that Malaysia would organise another Mount Everest expedition for climbers like me. Securing funds for climbing Mount Everest is also a very difficult task. I tried to do a charity climb called 'A dollar a step' to raise funds for AIDS but that ended in failure.

In the meantime, Mum and Dad were pressuring me to settle down soon. I would have turned down marriage proposals even if they came from millionaires. In fact I actually passed on my marriage proposal to my friend who was single. I really wanted a man who would understand, respect and accept me for who I was. I had a marriage proposal from this one guy whose family I knew. We met once and had dinner. I was quite open to talk about my Mount Everest dream. The next day, his mum rejected me, saying I would not be a committed wife for having a family! Even twelve years later, his mum asked my mum if I was still climbing mountains. It is a taboo for Asian girls and women to involve themselves in adventurous activities. Does that mean a woman cannot be a sailor, adventurer or space and galaxy explorer? I was quite disappointed by those remarks!

In the meantime, my younger brother moved to Australia and he could not keep up his mortgage payments. The mortgaging bank was after me, as guarantor, to settle the bills and threatened to blacklist me and to put the house up for auction. My dad and I were really stressed about this.

Climbing Books

I used to go to the National Library in Singapore with my friend Shanti to borrow books of climbing stories. I had to use her library card. I read a lot of books about climbing Everest. I read

Jon Krakauer's Into Thin Air many times.

Another book I read, in March 2003, was by Anatoli Boukreev and G Weston Dewalt: The Climb: Tragic Ambitions on Everest. Anatoli Boukreev was my idol. He was a Russian citizen and a resident of Almaty, Kazakhstan. He was considered one of the world's most successful high-altitude climbers. By spring 1996, he had climbed seven of the most challenging 8000 metre mountains, and all of them without oxygen supplementation.

The 'eight-thousanders' are the fourteen mountains whose height is more than 8000 metres (26,247 feet) above sea level. They are all located on the Himalayan and Karakoram mountain ranges. They are the mountains whose summits are in the 'death zone'. Death zone is the phrase used because it is believed that no human body can acclimatize at 8000 m as the oxygen level is insufficient to sustain human life. The fourteen mountains are Everest (8848 m), K2 (8611 m), Kangchenjunga (8586 m), Lhotse (8516 m), Makalu (8485 m), Cho Oyu (8201 m), Dhaulagiri I (8167 m), Manaslu (8163 m), Nanga Parbat (8126 m), Annapurna I (8091 m), Gasherbrum I (8080 m), Broad Peak (8051 m), Gasherbrum II (8035 m) and Shishapangma (8027 m).

One of Boukreev's quotes, "There is no room for mistake, you need good weather and very good luck", is a reminder to me as well.

I adored Boukreev's acclimatisation plan. I made a note of it and planned to use the same sort of plan on my future Everest climb.

In April 2003, I read a book written by Margo Chisholm and Rac Bruce: To The Summit.

The book fascinated me because Margo was a woman, like me.

She said, "A successful climb always depends on the consent of unseen powers." I thought for a moment, "How true that is when it comes to climbing! The two aboriginals who bought me pairs of rubber shoes were God-sent messengers!"

"Climbing feeds my soul in a way that nothing else does"; also the truth of me.

Heart to Heart Communication

Many may wonder why climbers undertake difficulties and struggles to hike for many days to reach a summit. The truth is to overcome personal limitations, and test their fitness and mental endurance. Beyond that, the beautiful scenery, high mountain ranges, the awesome view of sunrise and sunset will lure climbers from all over the world to go hiking for the rest of their life, once they fall in love with mountains.

No permanent job, no sign of a Mount Everest expedition, threatening letters from the mortgage company depressed me deeply despite training really hard.

I broke down in tears. I said to Mount Everest:

Sagarmatha, you are the mother of this earth and also a mother of my soul. I am your child. Is that wrong to have a dream? No mother will let her child down. My dearest mum, please open your door for me. Please accept me, open your arms widely for me, and hug me as tight as possible. Let me sleep on your lap and sing me a lullaby. Let me step on you, please give an opportunity, Ma, Sagarmatha – please show me unconditional love and say "yes" and show me a way to an Everest expedition!

NEW LIFE

In August 2003, I took my schoolchildren for a jungle trek. I received an e-mail from Karna in London just before leaving home. I was so curious about this new person. My friend Ahalli-yah, who was a nun at the Hare Krishna temple in Watford, gave my e-mail address to him just in case I would be interested in his profile.

As I was so distressed about the financial situation, I needed someone to talk to and he was there for me. We seemed to con-nect straight away and I first came to London in September 2003 for a week. In October 2003 my teaching contract came to an end and I decided to move to London. We got married the fol-lowing year. Our priority was to clear financial debt and transfer the house into my name. I always admire his strong negotiation skills, which was my biggest shortfall and I was not able to nego-tiate. Being an engineer himself, he fixed things after just reading manuals and instructions. I had rarely known people like him and I admired him for his engineering and technology skills. We both climbed Snowdonia in 2005 and Ben Nevis in 2006. He climbed successfully even though he was not a climber by himself.

I found it very difficult to understand the English accent and to get a job in this country. So he advised me to do a Sage accounting system course. In September 2004, I went to Enfield College to enquire about Sage and Mr John Bishop suggested I should do an Association of Accounting Technicians (AAT) course and Sage was part of it. After one week of college study, I managed to get a job as Accounts Assistant in a warehouse.

In the AAT class, again I had trouble answering questions in my class when Mr Bishop called my name. I e-mailed him and told him about the trouble that I had. He was the first person I had told about my speech impairment. When my turn came to answer, I looked at him, he acknowledged me and I smiled before

I could answer him. "That was a good technique about being open about my blocked speech problem to my tutor," I thought. Also, asking questions in class was very difficult for me as the word 'question' would stick in my mouth. So instead of saying, "I have a question", I changed my approach: "Can I ask you something?" That's how I dealt with my thirst for knowledge whether at college or work. This approach helped me to be the best in my class.

Then, I moved to another company for a year as Accounts Clerk. I decided to do English evening classes in City Lit College to improve my grammar and pronunciation. I met tutor David Buckam, who said that words could be said clearly if we practised moving our mouth muscles. I started to practise "What, where, when, why" by exercising my mouth muscles while I was cooking meals. That technique helped me too.

I managed to get a job in London Borough of Brent as a Finance Officer. I met new colleagues and kept in touch with some of my managers who left for a better career.

At work, I realised how important it was to be communicative in order to progress up the career ladder. Most colleagues that I have worked with have moved on to new jobs with better pay whereas I stayed in one place despite going for many interviews.

I wanted to go back to my climbing again. On weekends I used to go to a field to run. Suddenly, while running, I felt so sick and later I found out I was pregnant.

I completed AAT studies in 2007 and was awarded the MAAT qualification (full membership of the AAT) in 2008. I was pregnant with our first child. In November 2007, I enrolled for the CIMA qualification (Chartered Institute of Management Accountants). During my thirty-one weeks of pregnancy I started to feel pressure building up in my right ear. It was very difficult to sleep at night sometimes.

During maternity leave, I went to see my doctor. It was only in 2013 that an ear, nose and throat consultant confirmed that I have tinnitus in my right ear. I was really sad but I did not want to let go my dream. I asked the consultant if tinnitus would interrupt my climbing hobby. He answered very lightly, "No, and enjoy doing the things you like to do." It is true that when you are so passionate about achieving something nothing can stand in your way, and even if it does you will always a find a way around it to ultimately achieve your dream with God's blessing.

Reganathan

Reganathan was born on 24.2.2008 via emergency C-section. He was a beautiful baby boy. I enjoyed being Mum and being at home for the first five and a half months. During this time, I re-sat three CIMA exams and passed two papers. I remember carrying Regan on my shoulder while I studied for exams. I would speak CIMA theories out loud to Regan like a story.

My husband decided to be full time carer. I went back to work in August 2008. I missed Regan so much and wished I could have stayed at home a bit longer. Regan was underweight all the time.

On 23.12.2008 I returned home from work and was really tired on that night. Regan wanted his milk and I told my husband to get his milk for him. My husband gave him his milk in a bottle and carried Regan down the stairs thinking it would be easier to burp him. But he slipped and Regan fell from his arm and hit his head on the floor. My husband screamed before Regan cried and I will never forget that scream and those cries. I rushed down to see both. Regan's head was swollen straight away. We rushed to hospital and the X-ray and CT scan results showed he had a broken skull. I was extremely sad for poor little Regan but the doctor said the broken skull would heal naturally as he was under two years old. I stayed with him in the hospital. I stayed positive all the time. I know I am a self motivator and life would change forever after this. Like all mothers, I had a dream for my son while I was pregnant. I wanted him to be an astronaut and explore space. The doctors said we would not know what would happen, what impact the head injury would have on him. The paediatrician comforted me: "Regan is a miracle boy who survived a nasty head injury."

My manager, Neena Avinash Patel, with her family, visited us every alternate day and she would bring food for me. My other colleague, Joseph Emmanuel, would visit every other day too. I have no family in this country and I was really touched by their generosity to me. I have to admit that I am lucky to meet great people even though I had only few friends.

Also, after the hospital appointments, we found out Regan had delayed development and was not meeting the development milestones. I had to take him for occupational therapy appointments. Neena was really an understanding manager. She allowed me to take time off in the morning to attend Regan's various hospital appointments. I had great support from her that enabled me to stay focused on my day to day job. After returning from office work, I spent a lot of time with him and took him to the park and let him walk on the grass during the summertime. I remember holding his hands and slowly letting go his grip and he would stumble to stand straight. The first milestone he reached was at eighteen months when he walked. I would study at night time, after putting him to sleep.

I applied for a new role at work. I successfully got the new role.

My Dad is Very Ill

In September 2009, my dad was admitted into mental health hospital as he was very depressed. While he was at the hospital, he had a stroke and he was transferred to the General Hospital in Johor Bahru. The doctors resuscitated him. He was put on a life support machine and was told by doctors that he had only a little chance to survive. My mother rang me to visit Dad immediately. I have not even started on my new role yet. I informed my new manager. I took Regan with me to Malaysia. I prayed to God so hard to see Dad alive. That was the only wish that I wanted so badly at that moment.

I saw my dad in the life support machine and I got really emotional. His eyes were shut. He was unconscious. I looked at his face, tried holding my tears, and said to him, "Dad, your daughter Kala is here." He opened his eyes. I touched his arm and kissed his forehead and I said in my heart to him, "Dad – I cannot forget the days you punished me for my stammer in front of my class mates but I forgive you, I thank you for giving me a life, I love you forever and now I accept the destiny of my life!"

He smiled. I still remember his smile even though he did not know I was there for him. That was the last smile I saw on my dad's face.

I went back home. My dad usually planned his day by writing on a white board. He had written the word 'limp' on it. I thought he might have been depressed recently thinking about his physical limitation. Mum used to tell us that Dad had to take his tablets on time otherwise he would behave in a very strange way. I was so determined that night thinking Dad should live as he was fighting for life on a life support machine. I simply did not want to let him go.

I signed the consent form for him to have a tracheostomy when everyone in the family refused to do so. He survived and stayed nearly two months in hospital.

I got pregnant with a second baby in November 2009. My husband was stressed with the financial problems that we had.

On 24.5.2010 I received the distressing news that my dad had passed away. I cried so much and I was upset that I could not go to the funeral as I was pregnant. I had lost my dad forever and he would not even see my second son, whom he was looking forward to seeing.

Kevinathan

On 23.8.2010 Neena looked after Regan at Barnet hospital so that my husband could be with me during delivery. I gave birth to Kevinathan via planned C-section. The second boy of the family. He looked exactly like my dad; "What a surprise," I thought. Kevin is a constant reminder of my dad – a tiny little 'Ramachandran'!

Regan started to talk at the age of three-plus but he started to stutter and took a while to say 'wh' words. I learnt a few techniques from the British Stammering Association website. I really did not want Regan to stammer. I would never tell Regan that he stammers or stutters. I would never make him repeat any word or sentence either. I just encourage him to talk as much as possible. I give him the opportunities that I was not given to explore new words. He still stutters sometimes but he is becoming a chatterbox.

I took eight months' maternity leave and went back to work in June 2011. My communication with my husband broke down permanently and I tried all I could to keep the marriage together. Kevinathan was a bad sleeper and I had broken nights for three and a half years after he was born.

I knew I needed to be bold in talking. I always wanted to know the leadership styles of the Chief Executive of Brent. In October 2013, I put my name forward to meet my chief executive in a group lunch in which I had to introduce myself. Amazingly, for the first time, I did not have blocked speech. It was fluent. I have been confident ever since then that I can speak to someone at chief executive level.

In March 2014 I decided to break my marriage relationship. It was the toughest decision I have ever made in my life. My two boys are the greatest gift from my husband.

I left my family home with my two boys to start a new life and a new me in the New Year, 2015.

DREAM CHASER

The only way for me to deal with the separation was to go back to climbing again, besides focusing on Regan's skills as he still has delayed development.

The next big questions were where, when and how to start to chase my dream again as I was struggling with child care arrangements.

I finally thought about my aspiration and the connection to my stammer. I said to myself, I should do the Mount Everest charity climb for the British Stammering Association. The best way to start was by asking my employer to join the Employers' Stammering Network.

In September 2014, I kept looking at the LinkedIn profile of Leys Geddes – who is an ambassador of the British Stammering Association and also former chairman of the association. He sent me a message offering to assist me in any way he could. I e-mailed him my brief story. He said the charity climb would be really tough and I had set a very difficult task but I would have his moral support.

At work, my Operational Director of Finance, Mick, seemed to be an approachable, attentive listener with great leadership skills and I thought maybe he could make things work for me. He was the second man with whom I wanted to strike a conversation but this time it was about my stammer and aspiration. I tried a few times after work but I failed to bring up my intention.

On 03.12.2014, I e-mailed him that I would like to meet him. He agreed to this. I was really nervous to talk about it because no one at work knew about my stammer or my Everest dream. I am quiet but very much a results orientated person. I still remember getting up from my chair and saying to myself, "Kala – you have got to do this, now!" I thought of Nelson Mandela and Princess Diana to give me the courage and the strength they shared! I approached him.

I briefly spoke about my dream of thirty-one years and how I train my brain to use easy words. I could see from his face that he had sympathy for me. I e-mailed him the Employers' Stammering Network link. He e-mailed the Human Resources Director, who then forwarded the message to the Head of Equality Team. In the end, due to financial pressure in local authorities, they decided not to be a member but said they could provide all the support for staff who stammer. That was my initial step to be open with my employer about my speech impairment.

Khoo Swee Chiow

Sometime between 2000 and 2001, while going to work in Singapore one day I had picked up a free newspaper from MRT station. There was an article printed about Khoo Swee Chiow, Malaysian born Singaporean adventurer who was about to make a second attempt to conquer the North Pole. If he succeeded, Swee Chiow would be the fourth man in the world to complete the grand slam adventure. This consists of conquering the North and South Poles and climbing the world's tallest peak as well as the highest summit in each of the seven continents. His website address was given in the newspaper article.

I thought, "Let's approach him to express my dream, I must keep trying until I find someone to guide me through my Everest dream!" So, I e-mailed him and I was really delighted to get a reply from him.

I remember calling him once before leaving Singapore to come to England in 2003. He sounded very humble. He was the third public figure whom I had contact with.

Training for Everest Base Camp

I contacted DB Koirala from Kathmandu over the Christmas period. I confirmed the dates to trek from Kathmandu to Everest Base Camp from 3.5.2015 to 22.5.2015. I planned the dates based on 2015 Everest summit dates so that I would have opportunities to meet Everest climbers at Everest Base Camp. I also planned to meet Khoo Swee Chiow on 17.5.2015. That was my target date and it kept me motivated to train for Everest Base Camp.

I managed to get an au pair to look after the boys so that I could start my training in February 2015. I devised my own training plan – five days a week consisted of running around Wembley Stadium, as my office, Brent Civic Centre, was just next to the stadium, and also climbing up the stairs for nine floors up to five times at one go. I trained hard after work, which usually took about an hour. The Bobby Moore statue at Wembley Stadium inspired me to think about the strength and motivation within himself. I felt I was back to my normal being again.

I met Leys Geddes on 12.4.2015 at McDonald's, Waterloo Station. I have to admit that for the first time in my life, I did not feel nervous or have butterflies in my tummy. I felt I was meeting my kind of person. I felt so relaxed even during the meeting. He was very supportive. He posted a brief story of my intention in British Stammering Association (BSA) Facebook and I could see I was already getting support, from the members particularly.

On 16.4.2015 I received an e-mail from Swee Chiow to be safe and enjoy the mountain. I replied, 'I feel like I am coming to see my mother!' I was chanting "Om Mani Padme Hum", an auspicious mantra, in my heart whenever my mind was quiet in order to be blessed for the trek.

On 18.4.2015 I took a day off from work to climb Mount Snowdon – the highest mountain in Wales. I packed my climbing gear the night before and put it in the car before the boys woke up. I did not want to tell the boys that I was going to be away for a night. "They will stop me before they go to school," I thought. Aleida, the au pair, and I dropped the boys at school. After seven years, this was going to be the first night the boys had been left on their own with someone else. I wondered how they would cope. I bought an iPad for my trek to Skype with the boys and to capture pictures during the climb. I put the satellite navigation on and drove 222 miles to my destination. I felt I was going into an unknown world on my own. The drive within Snowdonia National Park was exceptionally beautiful, fascinating and amazing.

I reached Ffestiniog around 3.30 p.m. I booked into a hotel and Skyped with the boys for the first time. I thought, "This is how it is going to be when I go to Everest Base Camp for three weeks." I climbed Snowdon the following day and I captured many beautiful pictures. I felt a sense of pride doing the things I loved to do.

The weekends are always dedicated to the boys.

Earthquake in Nepal

25.4.2015: I rang DB Koirala – my Everest Base Camp trekking organiser at Kathmandu – at 6.46 a.m. UK time. I spoke to him for sixteen minutes to do my final checklist. I realised that I needed to buy a sleeping bag. After talking to him, I reserved a Hi Gear sleeping bag from the GO Outdoors online shop.

Around 10 a.m., the four of us got ready to go to the Science Museum. It was a great day out for us and I thought, "I am going to miss them a lot when I go to Kathmandu in a week's time."

We came back home around 3 p.m., rested for thirty minutes then got into the car and went shopping; we went to Colindale to get my sleeping bag.

I cooked my favourite chicken curry and before I had my dinner, I went online to check my e-mails. That's when I saw the news about the 7.8-magnitude earthquake that had struck Kathmandu and the Mount Everest region. I was completely shocked because I had spoken to DB only an hour before the massive earthquake. There are no words that can describe what would have happened if it had been the following week. The first thing to strike my mind was that my two boys would have been motherless! I don't want that to happen to them. I cuddled them as tight as possible and told them about the earthquake. I had not even made my will out for them yet! Not knowing the full extent of damage caused by the earthquake I was still thinking of going ahead with my plan.

I went to work on Monday and a lot of the colleagues that I spoke to said someone is looking after me for sure. I have to admit this is not the first time; I have escaped such a disaster before. In fact, my passion to climb Mount Everest still grows in me because it is my life and my climb is a charity climb to raise funds for the British Stammering Association. The climb itself will raise awareness of stammering and the funds raised will be channelled to BSA for them to carry on supporting the young ones who are affected by speech impairment.

On Monday night, my fellow climber Mr Chong pulled out from the climb. I e-mailed Swee Chiow that night for advice. His wife confirmed that he was safe and with his team mates and advised I should postpone until autumn 2015. I cancelled my flight bookings and had a confirmation that my full ticket price would be refunded in four to six weeks' time. I still carried on doing my stairs training for the following week. I told my colleagues that I would be going in autumn 2015.

The 7.8-magnitude earthquake on 25.4.2015 killed more than

8000 people according to official reports.

Unfortunately, on 12.5.2015 there was another earthquake, at 7.3-magnitude, that killed at least 110 people.

My colleague Lakshmi Varsani advised I should postpone it at least for a year. I took her advice and thought for a moment. I had been training really hard and I had to postpone for a year. But, my goal is Mount Everest. So, on 14.5.2015 I thought I should train in a different country. I chose Argentina and Mount Aconcagua (6962 metres). Swee Chiow told me he is organising a Mount Aconcagua expedition in January 2016. I expressed my interest to join his team.

My second planned face to face meeting with Swee Chiow was on 19.8.2015 at Yishun's McDonald in Singapore. He came with his wife, Wee Leng, to see me. He gave me a t-shirt as a present. He printed t-shirts to celebrate his success in conquering 100 peaks. The slogan on the t-shirt was 'If the mind is willing, the body will adapt'. "How true it is!" I said to both of them. We discussed training requirements, preparations for the Mount Aconcagua trip and personal challenges that I face as a working single mother and a climber.

Swee Chiow looked extremely confident, friendly, smiley faced, fit and lean. It was an amazing experience to meet someone who had earned the highest rewards in the mountaineering world, and who is also a public figure.

Personal Challenge

During the Mount Snowdon climb I had had intermenstrual bleeding. I thought it must be shock to my system as I had not done a single mountain climb in the previous nine years. However, the intermenstrual bleedings never stopped in the following months. I was worried thinking this was the time I needed my body to be fit for high altitude climbing but my body was not coping with strenuous training. I made a doctor's appointment and I told my GP about my future climbs as I have never had this symptom before. My blood test showed I had high calcium, low iron and low vitamin D.

I was sent for a scan. The first scanning results revealed that I have tiny fibroids in my uterus but my GP was not convinced that would have caused intermenstrual bleedings. My GP referred me for a second scan and to a gynaecologist. This time the scan showed I had a polyp and I was told the best way to stop the irregular bleeding would be to have a hysteroscopy done. On 10.11.2015 I went to Ealing hospital and hysteroscopy was performed under general anaesthetic in an operating theatre. The polyp was finally removed.

My training consisted of climbing up stairs and the usual walk from home to train station. I could only dedicate forty-five minutes to stair training three times a week. I set my personal target. Mount Aconcagua stands at 22,838 feet in height. I thought I should do at least 22,900 steps from November onwards before the actual climb. Unfortunately, I had to put my training on hold for three weeks after the hysteroscopy. When I felt slightly better, I restarted my training and I could only do 7560 steps in three weeks. I started to have a child care problem again and I stopped training from 12.12.2015. Now, the only training I could do was my usual fast walk from home to the train station and vice versa. I was quite worried as my training was not going according to plan.

I made an arrangement for my friend Besty to look after my kids while I was away for three weeks. But she informed me that she was not feeling too well. That left me with the biggest challenge ever – to look for a nanny. Besty suggested I try the childcare.co.uk website. I was searching actively for a nanny. I even asked my office colleagues if they could look after my kids for three weeks. This is when I made friends with Lisa. She lives near to my home. She was a carer by profession. She felt real sympathy for me when I could not find anyone. She decided to give me a

2015 - Snowdon summit

2016 - Mt Aconcagua Base Camp 4200m with Pasang Llamu Sherpa Akita

2016 - Day 3 in the morning near Casa de Piedra after river crossing

2016-Los Penintentes just above Mt Aconcagua Base Camp

contingency plan that she would do the school run for the boys and ask one of her sons' former tutors to help to look after my kids at home in the evenings and at night.

It was 23.12.2015. I still could not find a nanny. Caroline Davies, who has been a great supporter since my Everest Base Camp plan, asked me if I would cancel this expedition and I simply could not answer her and I was trying to control my tears. The next night after putting my two boys to sleep I broke into tears for hours. I simply did not want to give up and let go my dream. I was 100% sure that if I was not able to follow my dream then, I would never be able to in the future because I would face a similar sort of problem. I had paid a huge of amount of money for this expedition and heavily invested in climbing clothes, boots and gear. I searched and searched for a nanny from the website Besty suggested. I carried on looking actively even on Christmas Day. I made many phone calls. Finally, I Skyped, checked references, interviewed and selected Andrea as a live-in nanny for three weeks for my two boys. She started with us from 30.12.2015. I left the kids with her on 01.01.2016 to fly to Mendoza, Argentina. Even though I had only known her for less than three days, I had faith in her that she would care for my two boys selflessly. I also made plans for a few of my friends to visit the boys during the three weeks.

At Gatwick airport, Regan said, "Mummy, I love you, please take care." Kevin's face was a bit sad. "Mummy, I will miss you, safe journey, but don't get tired!" The two of them were the greatest force for me to return home safely after that expedition.

TREKKING TO ACONCAGUA

The team consisted of thirteen climbers, Rajan, Nigel, Neena, Michael, Joon Kai, Rajesh, Raja Bose, Joan, Kitti, Longjiang, Jing Luo (Maggie), Gujing and I, led by Swee Chiow with four guides, Pablo, Chacho, Coco and Herman. I only knew Swee Chiow, not the team members. This was an international expedition as there were UK, China, Singapore, Malaysia and Thailand nationals on this team. The climbers were experienced mountaineers. Most of them had already accomplished a minimum height of 5895 m (Mount Kilimanjaro), but I had not. Longjiang was an Everest summiteer. Michael had attempted Everest twice. Maggie had already completed seven of the 8000-metre high mountains and she is the second climber in ranking in China to accomplish 8000-m-high mountains.

There are two routes to the summit of Aconcagua. One is known as Vacas Valley Route and the other is known as Normal Route. It takes three days covering 42 km to Base Camp (4200 m) using the Vacas Valley Route. Swee Chiow's plan was to traverse the mountain from Vacas Valley to Horcones Valley.

On 03.01.2016 the four guides inspected our climbing gear in our hotel rooms. I had most of the climbing equipment except for sleeping bag, climbing helmet and ski goggles, which I intended renting. However, they did not notice that my down jacket had no hood. But they advised me to wear two top base layers if I felt cold. I had to fill in forms for a climbing permit. I noticed that one of the guides was holding a thermal flask and 'Argentinian' tea cup. "What's that?" I asked. They said it was called 'Mate'. It is a traditional tea which gives extra energy. They were probably surprised when I said I wanted to drink it too! It tastes like mildly bitter herbal tea. Moreover, I kept drinking three to four litres of water every day after I arrived at Mendoza. I was advised to drink plenty of water to minimise altitude sickness.

On 04.01.2016 we went to hire climbing clothes and equipment.

One of the problems we had from the start was that the luggage belonging to three Chinese nationals did not arrive at Buenos Aires airport. In Argentina only few speak English. Chacho and the three Chinese stayed back at the hotel and planned to fly to Buenos Aires to sort out their luggage and then join us on Aconcagua.

We left Mendoza at 1.10 p.m. for Punte de Inca by minibus. The road journey towards Punte de Inca was astonishingly beautiful. We reached Penitentes Cruz De Cana – a hotel near Punte de Inca – in the late evening. The altitude is 2250 metres. The rooms were really small. The bunk beds were tiny too. During dinner, Swee Chiow passed around his oximeter. The oximeter is a probe that can be attached to a finger to measure the pulse rate and the saturation level of oxygen in red blood cells. For a healthy person at sea level, an oximeter reading should be in the range of 96–98%. At 6000 metres, a reading of 75–80% is a sign of good acclimatization. The higher we climb, the lower the oximeter reading is on arrival, but as we acclimatize at higher altitude, the oximeter reading should increase. A low reading is a warning for altitude sickness. My oximeter reading was only 80 at this altitude and others' were higher than mine.

On 05.01.2016 I woke up with a light headache on the left side of my head. I had my breakfast with others. We were advised to carry water bottles, trekking poles, down jacket, shell jacket, dry snack, lunch pack in our day backpack. Other climbing gear and clothes were packed in duffel bags to be transported by mules to the next campsite, Pampa de Lenas – 2800 metres. We left the hotel and were driven in a minibus to the entrance of the park. It was a beautiful day at Vacas entry point with clear blue sky but windy. I wore a wide brimmed hat and sunglasses to prevent sun burn and sand dust going into my eyes. We started our first day hike up at 11.45 a.m. We walked up the mountain west of Vacas

River. The water current was fast and we could hear just the noise of the river. The first day hike was about fourteen kilometres. The Andes offers only limited vegetation. I saw hardy grasses, yellow wild flowers and low flying tiny little birds on the way. There is plenty of open space to enjoy the beautiful view. It was moderate walking on big rocks. It rained on and off; with a shell jacket on, it was a battle between feeling hot and keeping warm while trekking up to Pampa de Lenas. After a few hours of walking, our mules overtook us and we needed to give way to mules for them to pass by. At some point, there was a danger of rockfall due to mules passing by. However, this was the first time I had used trekking poles for climbing and I felt so uncomfortable walking with the poles. My team mates were faster than me. All of sudden I felt a sharp pain in my right leg. I could not even lift my leg up and move forward. I slowed down and put away my trekking poles. I told Pablo that my right leg was aching and I thought I had strained it. He slowed down for me. I must have taken six hours plus to reach Pampa de Lenas. I was thirty minutes later than the rest of the team. I told the team that I might have pulled my right leg muscle. I put up my tent with others and helped others to pitch their tent too. Coco advised me to stretch my legs to flex my right leg muscle. We had dinner but the guides offered me only vegetarian food. The guides had misunderstood my dietary requirement. Swee Chiow had told them that I do not eat beef but they had misunderstood and thought me vegetarian. I learnt a very important lesson here, that I should check what foods are on offer at each camp site beforehand so as to avoid 'lost appetite' and get the right food for climbing. The guides apologised and offered me pork sausages instead of beef barbecue. I saw a humble Sherpa lady here and I thought she was a cook as she was cooking for her expedition mates. That night Coco advised me to stay at his pace for the second day's hike. Rajan said he would trek with me.

On 06.01.2016, in the morning, Rajan massaged my right leg. He said my leg was swollen. I screamed when he pressed my vein. Swee Chiow gave me an anti-inflammatory tablet. We had to hike fifteen kilometres up to Vacas Valley. There were smaller rivers to cross and moderate walking on rocks. The weather is unpredictable here. The sunshine was really strong but it was quite windy and the wind carried the sand dust up and blew it into my face. I covered my mouth with my balaclava to avoid sand dust going into my mouth. I learnt from Coco to use a rhythmic slower pace when climbing up and a faster pace when climbing down. Coco reminded me to drink water only at rest areas as I kept drinking water all the way up as I was out of breath most of the time. The view was amazingly beautiful. I enjoyed the company of Rajan and Coco during my Day 2 on Aconcagua. Thank God, the massage eased my pain in the leg. After several of hours walking, we reached a wide open area called Casa de Peidra (House of Stone) plateau. Coco pointed out Cerro Ameghino mountain (5883 metres) from there, north east of Aconcagua, just before reaching our campsite. If the weather is clear, one can catch a glimpse of Aconcagua from there.

Finally, after seven hours of walking, still I was the slowest one, being one hour behind the rest of the team in arriving at the beautiful but windy Casa de Piedra (3200 metres) campsite. I pitched my tent with the help of Coco and other climbers. I simply liked this campsite.

After a tasty dinner that night, I spent time talking with the humble lady had I met at Pampa de Lenas. She is Pasang Llamu Sherpa Akita, then nominated for 2016 People's Choice Adventurer of the Year by the National Geographic Society. She advised me to drink four to five litres of water during the day for better acclimatization. She was the first one in two days of trekking to say, "This mountain is very beautiful." I looked up the sky. Wow! The sky was full of stars, I have never seen that many stars, looking so close, anywhere before. Herman said the constellation I spotted was Orion. The star gazing was a feast for my eyes for many nights during my stay.

On 07.01.2016 Rajan massaged my leg again. He said he could not follow my pace and would like to follow his own pace. Coco asked me to stay at the front of the team if I could do so so that I could be at the same pace as the others. We had to go on mule to cross a river before starting our twelve-kilometre hike to Plaza Argentina (4200 metres), which is the base camp of Aconcagua. The trail was a quite narrow, steep, sandy path and rocky too. There is a danger of rock fall there. However, I had to breathe deeper and I felt I was out of breath and had less energy to hike up. I saw my fellow climbers having lunch. I sat down and for the first I had a glimpse of Aconcagua summit when the cloud cleared. After I had rested for about twenty minutes, we started to climb again. I could not hike as fast as the others. My throat started to hurt and I felt thirsty most of the time. Herman stayed with me. I kept asking how long to go. He must have been annoyed at one point. I relied on my Suunto watch to check the altitude. I had to rest a couple of minutes for every ten paces. I was disappointed with my fitness level at that time. I saw Coco coming down towards me when we were just 100 metres from the base camp. He asked if I was okay. I said, "I am just too tired!" He took away my backpack and told me we were quite near. I was very touched with his act of kindness. I reached the Base Camp two hours behind the rest of the team. It was freezing cold. Raja Bose gave me hand warmers as I walked into the mess tent. Everyone's eyes were on me. Only I knew how frustrated and disappointed I was at that time. Swee Chiow told me to check my oximeter reading. It was only 66 on arrival. He gave me one tablet of 250 mg Diamox and advised me to drink plenty of water. Someone pitched my tent for me. It was too windy and too cold. The strong wind's howling noise kept me awake the whole night.

The following day was a rest day. I was at the mess tent after breakfast. When I came out, I saw my tent was upside down and Pablo was holding it. Herman came and I held my tent while he went to look for big rocks to secure it. Thank God my tent had not flown away.

During the rest day, Swee Chiow and other guides showed us how to fix crampons onto our mountaineering boots. My mountaineering boots, La Sportiva, were the most expensive item I have ever purchased for this expedition. I did practise wearing them at home a week before the expedition so that I could get used to the weight. We practised walking a while with the boots at Base Camp.

Raja Bose lent me his satellite phone. I had not spoken to my boys since 04.01.16; quite a while. The reception was not very good but at least I heard their voices. They were very excited to talk to me.

The lunch served was tortellini pasta with tomato sauce. I had tea and biscuit for afternoon tea. But I threw up when I went to Base Camp's toilet as it was dirty and smelly.

In the late afternoon, we went to the medical hut for a medical check-up. The medical check-up is quite strict on Aconcagua. The doctors can turn down climbers if any abnormality is present in oximeter reading, heartbeat, blood pressure and so on. My turn came. The doctor asked me, "When was the last time you climbed a mountain?" I answered, "Last April – Mount Snowdon in Wales." He asked how high it is and I said, "It is about a thousand metres." He joked that it is only a hill! He checked my oximeter reading. It was 77. He told to return for a medical check-up again the next morning before attempting Camp 1. If I could maintain it at 77, he would give me the go ahead…

Also, Longjiang and Maggie joined us at Base Camp as they started later than us. They did three days' trek up in just two days. They were super fit and superfast!

Gujing returned to China as one piece of his luggage did not arrive at Buenos Aires. It was sad but maybe this trip in this season was just not meant for him!

That night the dinner was pizza with salami. I had a hard time even to swallow the food. My throat hurt. I went back to my tent to sleep. It had been cold and windy all day along. I started to shiver, so I quickly took two packs of hand warmers and placed them in between my summit mittens. I placed my hand on them and I felt slightly warmer. I lay down in my sleeping bag. However, I felt the food that I had just had coming up into my throat and down again to my stomach. I had never had such a problem before. I thought it may go away. But it kept happening. I thought, "How am I going to Camp 1 tomorrow?" I got up from my sleeping bag. I could not ignore even a small health problem. I am a mother and I have huge responsibility for my two boys. I said, "Regan and Kevin – looks like Mummy cannot join the rest of the team to Camp 1 tomorrow! Health and safety is more important than anything else and I need to fix my body right now!" I put on my down jacket, shell jacket, trekking boots and headed to the mess tent. I saw Rajan, Rajesh and Kitti there. I told them I was not feeling well and having reflux. One of them called the guides. Chacho, Coco, Herman and Pablo quickly came to see me. Coco gave me a nausea tablet and told me to put it under my tongue to dissolve it. Pablo gave me two cups of herbal tea. They started talking about helicopter evacuation if I did not feel well the next day. Then, it was decided that I should not sleep on my own to ensure I was safe throughout the night. So, Rajesh came with his sleeping bag and mat to my tent.

The next morning when I woke up I told Rajesh how physically unprepared I was for this mountain.

After breakfast, we went for a medical check-up again. This time my oximeter reading was 83. That was great news and in fact the reading had improved after two days! I told about the reflux and I was given two gastric pills and advised to take one tablet if I had reflux. However, I had decided not to join the team for Camp 1 on that day because of the pain in my throat.

The group left for Camp 1 at 11.30 a.m. However, Rajesh, Neena and Joon Kai returned with Coco in the late afternoon. They did not reach Camp 1 as it was windy and cold. The rest reached Camp 1.

At night time, I asked Swee Chiow and the guides if they could take me to Camp 1 the following day. They were quite concerned about my fitness level. I was disappointed at that time. I insisted that they take me at least two hours' hike up as I really wanted to see penitentes. Swee Chiow agreed to my request. That was when I sadly decided to leave Aconcagua and determined to work on my fitness level when I returned to London.

On 10.01.2016 after lunch time, Swee Chiow led me slightly above Base Camp to catch the first sight of los penitentes as per my request. Penitentes are icicles or pinnacles of snow formed by wind and sun. These are unique as you can find them in South American high altitude mountains. I saw some rock climbers climbing up as it was a very fine and beautiful day. Suddenly, I saw a man coming towards us. Swee Chiow knew him and introduced me. He had a water bottle and I asked if I could drink his water as I was very thirsty. He gave it and it tasted like my home water back in London. It tasted like a lemon drink. He was Jason Black, the famous Irish mountaineer and adventurer from Donegal, Ireland. I was lucky to meet him there. He visited us in our mess tent and chatted with all the other climbers too.

Even though I decided not to trek up further, I have brought back great memories of networking with world class mountaineers.

On 12.01.2016, Rajesh, Michael, Raja Bose and Joan trekked to further camps.

Raja Bose definitely came to this mountain with a big mission. He proposed marriage to Joan at Camp 1. He wished to do this on her birthday on 15.01.2016, which was our planned summit date, but both of them aborted their plan to join the summit team. Joan was very touched by his proposing to her at very high altitude and had tears of joy when she showed us the engagement ring. Both of them are experienced hikers and a happy couple!

Michael and Rajesh reached as far as Camp 2 and returned safely.

The season was El Nino season. Many climbers aborted their summit plan simply because the wind gusts were too strong and there was too much snow.

Apart from that, climbers being evacuated by helicopter because of injury, pulmonary oedema or other health issues were an unavoidable scene at Base Camp during my stay.

Nigel, Maggie, Long and Kitti decided to stay on the mountain for the summit push. The rest decided to head down as the weather was not great. However, Nigel's blood pressure was high and he was evacuated by helicopter the following day in the early morning. It must have been a great disappointment for a healthy climber like him.

On 13.01.2016, after spending six nights at an altitude of 4200 metres, we descended to Casa de Peidra. This time I could stay at team fitness level. It was the same route as on Day 3 but the descent was a lot easier for me mainly because Coco shared my backpack load. We had to cross a few rivers and we finally reached the last river before Casa de Peidra campsite. I asked Coco if he could pick up a pebble for me. He picked one and said to me, "Kala, next time when you return to this mountain, you are going to put this pebble on the summit of Aconcagua." He has given me a new commitment to return. I took the pebble from him and I said, "Well, I will try, Coco!" He continued, "There is no rush, when you are trained well, do come back."

We took the mule ride option to get back to Punta de Lenas. It was a seven hour bumpy mule ride. It was not a joke but the mules were very competitive. They were trying to overtake one another. I fell off once from the mule, which was a giggling scene for others.

My thighs were sore. Everyone walked like a robot that night after the mule ride.

The three who stayed on the mountain summited Aconcagua on 17.01.2016 and Pasang and her team members summited on 18.01.2016 when the weather was great for a summit push.

Pasang has now been awarded 'Adventurer of the Year 2016' by the National Geographic Society for her selfless contribution during Nepal's deadliest earthquake in history last year.

Looking back at my performance and my experience, I learnt lessons from this mountain – where I went wrong and what to do for the next expedition and what to look for in a commercial expedition like this. But, two things we cannot change are the weather and the mountain itself!

Nevertheless, I brought back great memories of Aconcagua. This is maybe just a beginning for a new journey in my life.

ANXIETY IN MAKING CONVERSATION

One of the toughest challenges faced by a person who stammers is the inability to hold conversations as a result of anxiety and stress, as well as tension. I was in many situations, especially in my school and university days, where I was not able to hold a very long conversation simply because of the fear of talking and the anxiety it created. I even run out of ideas of what to talk about sometimes when in a larger group. I hate being in that sort of situation.

I practised talking a lot in front of a mirror whenever I had to go for interviews. Practice builds up confidence and minimises the anxiety of having a conversation.

When I first started to work, I had to liaise with customers and suppliers over the phone. I usually wrote down the points I needed to talk about on a piece of paper to avoid to calling them again.

As a mother, I constantly talk to my two boys at home and feel that I am conversing a lot more now than before having kids!

If you are parent or a carer, encourage your child to speak. It may be frustrating for a parent to listen to blocked speech or stuttering or stammering but just imagine how much frustration and anxiety the child would go through at such a tender age. Cuddle and comfort them to show that you are very interested to hear what they are trying to say. Every child matters and no child should be left alone to deal with a stammer without any support and early intervention with speech and language therapy. It is cruel when a parent or carer ignores a child's basic foundation of communication. Most of the children who have an early intervention will grow out of stammering.

If you are a friend of a stammerer, listen to their conversation carefully and attentively without bullying them. Compliment them for their effort and make them feel comfortable with what they want to say. Let them speak for themselves and never finish their sentence for them. They are the only one who knows what they want in their lives.

If you are a teacher, stand up against bullies to support a student who stammers, encourage the child to be brave to initiate conversation and refer them to therapy sessions, if they are not attending them already, so that they are well supported from the beginning.

If you are a partner, spouse, husband or wife of a stammerer, instead of criticising, show them the support, care and love which will benefit the long term relationship.

If you are manager, a stammerer should be treated non-discriminatorily and equally to non-stammerers. Opportunities such as managerial roles, leading a project, organising events should be given to them at in the workplace to build their confidence amongst their colleagues. They are resilient, they have great problem solving skills and are full of hidden talent. A work team should represent a diverse work force as everyone has different skills to contribute to a productive and successful team.

Patience is vital for the listener. Anyone and everyone around a stammerer will need to play a courageous part to include and encourage them to make conversation. An inclusive and participative environment contributes to healthy wellbeing and makes this planet a better place to live in as a whole.

The Art of Talking

Carolyn Downs was appointed as our new Chief Executive in Brent. On 06.10.2015, she visited our floor and had a chat with every employee present. Minesh Patel (Acting Head of Finance) accompanied her. I had been thinking of her recently, on how to approach her to invite her along for my upcoming book launch. Now, she was there. I thought I had overcome my fear but my heart was beating so fast. So, I tried to be calm and patient. The two of them stood next to me. I stood up too to give eye contact to both of them. I wanted to say, "My name is Kala" but, the 'my' refused to come out of my mouth, and within a few seconds, I changed it to "I am Kala." Then, we shook hands and my speech was fluent with regard to my current work and it was an interactive conversation. At the end, Carolyn said, "Thanks, Kala." I thought that was great, simply because she remembered my name. The next day I sent an e-mail directly to her as advised by Minesh about my book launch. She replied that she would be pleased to help me in any way she could. Besides talking, I realised how important it is to have good body language and a good level of eye contact in order to impress someone at the first opportunity no matter to whom we are speaking. My dream of Mount Everest made me the person I am now, from timid to bold, from quiet and reserved and from introvert to extrovert.

Good communication skills play a very important role in expressing views, whether it is at home, work or company you are visiting. Having good communication skills encourages participation, understanding, empathy, negotiation and managing conflicts, and it avoids depression and isolation.

I still struggle with managing conflicts. I get really stressed and always feel heat on my face and feel pressure building up in my right ear because of my tinnitus. My approach is to withdraw from heated argument as much as possible. I know that is my physical limitation but I cannot blame my pregnancy with Regan. He is my first, gifted child, who is very kind towards me. He is very positive, a self motivator even though he had delayed development for many years. He amazed me when he first climbed Bukit Teresek on 22.8.2015 – the same hill that I climbed first in 1991.

Since I started to stammer, I have admired people who talk politely and passionately with a rich vocabulary of words.

Good communication skills provide a strong foundation in many aspects of life: childhood, business, education, employment and human relationships.

Fear of communication limits choices in life. It is worse when you do not do anything about it.

The only way to handle this is to be fearless when talking to someone. The starting point would be to choose someone whom you are comfortable with, who respects you and does not laugh or bully when you talk to them. Talk to them about your dream and feel the joy and you will realise that eventually the fear you feel when you are talking to someone will fade. It is also 'OK' to stammer. The moment you accept this, making and engaging in conversation with others will become a lot easier. Stammering will not go away but at least you will feel confident to talk to anyone and at any level.

Therapy is one of the best treatments, especially for a child. But, I believe it is never too late to have the right therapy you require at any age. Keep a record of what makes you feel nervous or makes you fearful and discuss it with your therapist.

Practice makes perfect. Keep practising words and sentences. This will boost self- confidence, self-esteem and self-motivation.

YOU ARE NOT ALONE

Stammerers easily fall into being bullied. Do not let anybody bully you. It is very important to know that what matters is not how we talk but the message the recipient gets. We have acts like the Equality Act 2010 that protect stammerers. There is a lot of network support available to employers to support stammerers. Never give up your dream simply because you have an invisible or visible disability or even mental illness!

The world now is a better place to live. The world and the universe still hold lots of mystery waiting to be explored. Thanks to the technology that we have. We have great living legends like Stephen Hawking, Bill Gates, Richard Branson, Barack Obama, Sir Chris Hoy, Sir Bradley Wiggins, JK Rowling, Hillary Clinton, Sir Chris Bonington and many more on the list, inspiring the world every second. The truth is, it could be anybody, even your family, friends, colleagues, teachers or kids that inspire you. We have resources and there should be no excuses that stop our genuine dream coming true, even if it is only a small dream. Everyone has talent. You are the only one who knows who you are. The talent will be wasted if not tapped. You are not alone in this world and life.

We just have to accept wholeheartedly our shortcomings that are invisible to others. It could even be a phobia or an addiction that harms your personal growth. Being open about your shortcomings is the best thing you can do for your own self. Don't be unkind to yourself. Get the right support you need from your family, friends, colleagues or anyone whom you can trust and are comfortable talking to. Believe me, ultimately you will find that one person who will say, "It's your time to be successful" if only you are ready to break your silence. There is nothing wrong in saying "I am a covert stammerer" or "I have an impairment" or "I have an addiction" even though there is a stigma about it! I hid my stammer for twenty-seven years, but not any more. Hurdles, hazards, negative comments, negative energy, failure, rejections will be on your way, but never surrender your dream just because they are thrown at you. Believe me, they are the best teachers to guide you to become strong, positive and confident while on your way to touch your dream.

There is a purpose in life: find it, go for it, try it, do it and succeed in it. The very important message about searching for the purpose of life is that you must never harm any living being physically, emotionally or mentally, not even in your thoughts. There is no shortcut to being successful. You will be blessed when you are ready to take on the challenge! Let your dream lead your passionate life with family, friends and others. Compliment yourself even on small achievements. Even if you don't succeed, the process of achieving through your dream is well worth it because there is only one life to live on this Mother Earth, and that life is short, so live fully! You will soon realise that self-confidence, self-esteem, persistence, structured approach, consistency and better communication skills will ultimately be your personality traits.

What-if

I do think of what-if questions sometimes.

What-if my dad had not had mental illness?
What-if my dad had not punished me?
What-if Regan had not had the fall?

The effects and consequences are just beyond our control and in my case this is what I called destiny.

Winston Churchill once said "a pessimist sees the difficulty in every opportunity; an optimist sees the opportunity in every difficulty."

Richard Branson positively said a pessimist is someone who is waiting to be an optimist.

Life is only beautiful and meaningful if you have courage, strong determination, perseverance, consistency, a 'can do' attitude, a passionate purpose in life, a great support network and, most importantly, a 'belief in yourself'.

A POEM OF COMFORT

I have a Friend
He is God
He is Eternal
He rescues me
He will not drown me
In the sea of a sorrow

I have a Friend
He is God
Have I seen you?
Yes I have
Through humans
And five elements of nature

I have a Friend
He is God
He is the Protector
He saves me from Evil

I have a Friend
He is God
He is my Cure
He is my Answer

2016 - With Reganathan on Snowdon, this picture was taken by Kevinathan

Lightning Source UK Ltd.
Milton Keynes UK
UKOW01f0133151016

285299UK00002B/83/P